**Kitchen Kreations**
collection

# The Ultimate Deep Fryer Recipe Collection

D0107970

# Table of Content

## *Appetizers & Snacks*

## *Dinners*

## Desserts

## Oddities

# Introduction

There is no arguing that people all over the globe love deep fried foods. It's hard to resist the delicious taste of deep fried onion rings, french fries, hush puppies, or a favorite treat such as a deep fried Twinkie or ice cream.

The good news is that there is no big secret to being able to deep fry great tasting appetizers, desserts, snacks and meals. All you need are a few of the basics to get started, along with the right recipes to go by. This book has you covered on both levels. It provides you with everything you need to begin cooking your favorite foods immediately.

We have designed all of our deep fried recipes to not only be fun to eat, but to be easy to make as well. Most of the ingredients you'll need are already in your kitchen, and that aren't available at any grocery store. We've also added recipes that are favorites in places all over the world, so you can enjoy your old favorites, in addition to trying new ones you may have never heard of before.

We've even included a section on deep fried oddities that you will want to check out. These are some of the most bizarre and unique recipes you'll find anywhere.

# The Basics Of Deep Frying

## Oil

Using the right type of oil is essential in creating great tasting foods in your deep fryer. It's a fact that not all oils cook alike, or give your foods the same flavor.

Our recommended oil for deep frying is peanut oil. It is the oil of choice for most pros as it has a higher smoking point and lasts quite a bit longer than other types of oil such as vegetable oils.

That said, many of today's restaurants use an oleic canola oil. That works very well, but it is not necessary for home cooking use. Not only that, but it can be hard to find and is more expensive.

## Deep Fryer Temperatures

Frying your foods at the right temperature is the key to having foods your family will love.

If you fry foods in oil that is not hot enough, you get foods with oil that has soaked into them. Deep fry them at temperatures that are too high and you get well done foods on the outside... and uncooked on the inside.

We have listed out the temperatures to use for each recipe. If you stick to theses recommended temps you will experience the best results.

In all cases, always follow the recommended temperature guidelines for your particular deep fryer. In most cases, all of the recipes call for temps in the 350 -400 degree F range.

## Replacing Your Oil

We get questions all the time from our readers in regards to how long the oil will last in their deep fryer before it needs to be changed. It varies of course due to how often you use your deep fryer or what type of oil you are using. But here are some quick and easy things to look for:

Foods begin to turn darker than normal, and they turn color much quicker
You notice the oil smoking at normal cooking temperatures
The oil begins to smell
Oil starts foaming while cooking

In restaurants they will strain the oil or run it through a filter. For home use we recommend simply replacing the oil. The end result will be much better tasting foods.

## Choose The Right Size Deep Fryer Or Frying Pot

We can't say this too often; always choose the right size of deep fryer or frying pot, cast-iron Dutch oven, etc. Hot oil can quickly catch fire if it begins to spill over.

Something you will notice when you go out shopping for a deep fryer is how most of them are small or have narrow openings for your food. They simply do not have the capacity to hold much food for frying. What that means to you is that if you are cooking for a family, look for the larger deep fryers or use much larger pots.

## Fill The Fryer With The Right Amount Of Oil

We often hear of fires and accidents in the kitchen from fryers that overflowed due to having way too much oil in them. Always fill the deep fryer with the recommended amount of oil. Do not overfill in any circumstances.

As a rule of thumb, always leave at least 3 inches between the top of the oil and the top of the fryer pot. That allows the oil to bubble normally without overflowing. It also allows the necessary room for the weight of the food being cooked.

## Quick Safety Tips

Keep the oil temperatures within the manufacturer guidelines.

Always use a deep fryer that has a temperature gauge built in. Some older models do not have them.

Keep water out of the oil or it will spatter out of the fryer, resulting in potential eye and skin injury.

Fingers should always be kept away from hot oil. Be sure to use a fryer basket to lower and remove foods. Use a slotted spoon, wooden spoon or tongs to turn foods over that are frying or remove them from the fryer.

Do not overload the fryer with too much food. Cook in small batches to avoid overcrowding. Not only will overloading be a safety issue, but your foods will not cook properly as well.

Always allow the oil to cool down to room temperature before moving it or discarding it. Most burns occur due to hot oil being spilled out while moving the fryer.

# Appetizers
# &
# Snacks

# Chicago Style Fried Mozzarella Cheese Sticks

## Ingredients

16 oz. mozzarella cheese
1/2 cup water
1/2 teaspoon garlic powder
1/2 teaspoon dried oregano, crushed
1/2 teaspoon dried parsley, crushed
1/3 cup cornstarch
3 large eggs, beaten
1 1/2 cups Italian seasoned breadcrumbs
2/3 cup all-purpose flour
1/8 teaspoon salt
1/8 teaspoon pepper

## Directions

Heat oil in deep fryer to 400 degrees F.

Next, you will need 3 medium sized bowls.

In first bowl, beat in the 3 eggs and add the water. Mix together and set it aside on counter.

In second bowl, add the breadcrumbs and then combine in the garlic powder, parsley oregano, as well as the salt and pepper. Stir until mixed. Set it aside.

In the third bowl, combine the flour and cornstarch and quickly stir.

Next, take the mozzarella cheese and cut it into individual strips. Optionally, you can also cut the cheese into circles or any other shape you desire.

Dip the cheese strips or shapes into the egg bowl, and then dip them into the breadcrumbs, followed by a quick dip in the flour. Repeat the process a second time. Double dipping provides the best results.

Add the cheese sticks to deep fryer and fry until they become a nice golden brown color. Remove from fryer and set on paper towels to drain before serving.

Makes approximately 4-6 servings.

# All In One Fried Cheese Balls

## Ingredients

10 oz. diced chicken breasts
3 slices bacon (Diced)
salt and pepper to taste
1/2 teaspoon dried parsley
1/2 cup shredded parmesan cheese
1 tablespoon mayonnaise
3 teaspoons plain flour
3/4 cup breadcrumbs

## Directions

Cook the chicken and bacon and then dice before mixing together in a large bowl. Add in a bit of salt and pepper along with the cheese, parsley, mayonnaise and flour. Stir together thoroughly.

Next, form the mixture into small balls approximately one-inch in diameter. Take the balls and run them through the bread crumbs. Place all of them in another large bowl. Refrigerate for 60-90 minutes.

Heat oil in deep fryer to 360 degrees F.

Remove the balls from the refrigerator and place in deep fryer. Fry for 9-10 minutes or until they turn golden brown. Remove and drain on paper towels before serving.

Makes approximately 3-4 servings.

# Deep Fried Zucchini Strips

## Ingredients

1 medium zucchini 8 inches long
2 large eggs, beaten
2 tablespoons whole milk, homogenized
3/4 cup all-purpose flour
1/2 teaspoon seasoning salt
3/4 cup cracker crumb (saltines)
1 (2 oz.) package béarnaise sauce mix

## Directions

Heat oil in deep fryer to 360 degrees F.

Rinse and clean off zucchini before cutting into 3 inch long pieces that are approximately 1/2 inch thick.

Combine the milk and eggs in a medium sized bowl and thoroughly mix together.

In a one-gallon food storage bag, toss in the season salt and flour and shake until mixed.

In another gallon food storage bag, drop in the cracker crumbs. (cornflakes can be used as a substitute)

Next, take the zucchini pieces and dip into egg bowl. Then place them in the flour bag and toss until well coated.

Repeat the process by dipping them into the egg bowl, but then add them to the cracker crumb bag and shake until coated.

Drop several zucchini pieces in deep fryer and fry for 2 minutes or until they just begin to turn a light golden color. You do not want to overcook the pieces. Remove from fryer and place on paper towels to drain before serving.

These taste great with béarnaise sauce that you can mix according to the package directions.

Makes approximately 4 servings.

# Max's Deep Fried Mushrooms

## Ingredients

8 -10 oz. whole white mushrooms
3/4 cup all-purpose flour
2 eggs, slightly beaten
1 cup Italian seasoned breadcrumbs

## Directions

Heat oil in deep fryer to 375 degrees F.

Take the mushrooms and wash them off while also removing the stems. Dry off as much of the water as you can by simply patting them down with a paper towel.

Add the flour to a small bowl. Add the eggs in another small bowl. Then have a third bowl for the breadcrumbs.

Dip the mushrooms in the flour just until coated. Then, place them in the egg bowl and finally, run them through the breadcrumbs.

Set them on a baking sheet or a few plates so that the batter can dry just a bit.

Add a small batch to deep fryer and fry for approximately 3 1/2 minutes or until you notice them turning golden brown. Remove from fryer and place on paper towel before serving.

Makes approximately 4 servings.

# Classic Deep Fried Onion Rings

## Ingredients

1 large onion, cut into 1/4-inch slices
1 1/4 cups all-purpose flour
1 teaspoon baking powder
1 teaspoon salt
1 egg
1 cup milk, or as needed
3/4 cup dry bread crumbs
Seasoned salt to taste

## Directions

Heat oil in deep fryer to 365 degrees F.

On a cutting board, slice the onion into 1/4 inch slices and then separate them into individual rings.

Add the flour, salt and baking soda in a small bowl and stir until mixed.

Run the onion rings through the flour mixture and be sure to coat them well before setting aside for the moment.

Next, in the same flour bowl, beat in the egg and pour in the milk. Stir until the mix becomes a nice batter. A fork works very well for mixing with this recipe.

Take the onion rings and dip them into the batter. Hold them up with a fork for a couple of seconds to drain off excess batter, or use a rack. Then, put the breadcrumbs on a plate or baking sheet. Gently place the onion rings onto the crumbs and tap them down to make crumbs stick before flipping them over to coat both sides.

Place 3-4 rings in fryer basket in fry for 3 minutes or until you see them become golden brown. Remove from fryer and place on paper towels. Add salt to taste before serving.

Makes approximately 3 servings.

# California Fried Artichoke Hearts

## Ingredients

2 eggs
1/2 cup milk
1 (15 oz.) can artichoke hearts, drained and quartered
1 1/2 cups seasoned dry bread crumbs
1/4 cup grated Parmesan cheese for topping

## Directions

Heat oil in deep fryer to 350 degrees F.

Prepare artichoke hearts. Get out 2 small bowls. In the first one, add the breadcrumbs. In the second one, mix together the eggs and milk. Stir well.

Take artichokes and first dip into the egg bowl, then place in breadcrumbs and coat well.

Add artichokes to deep fryer and fry 2-3 minutes. The artichokes should be golden brown in color. Remove and place on paper towels before serving along with the parmesan cheese.

Makes approximately 8 servings.

# Game Day Boneless Chicken Strips

## Ingredients

2 cup unbleached all-purpose flour
4 teaspoons salt
1 teaspoon ground black pepper
1 teaspoon cayenne pepper
1/2 teaspoon garlic powder
1 teaspoon paprika
1 egg
1 cup milk
3 skinless, boneless chicken breasts, cut into 1/2 inch strips
1/4 cup hot pepper sauce
1 tablespoon butter

## Directions

In a large bowl, mix in the flour, garlic powder, paprika, cayenne pepper, salt and black pepper and quickly stir.

In a separate small bowl, beat in the egg and add the milk. Stir until mixed together well.

Take the chicken strips and dip each one in the egg bowl. Then, put them in the flour mixture. Repeat the process again so that each strip has been double-dipped. It will give you the best results. Finally, put the strips in your refrigerator for 15 minutes.

While chicken is in the refrigerator, heat oil in deep fryer to 375 degrees F.

Remove chicken from refrigerator and place a small batch in deep fryer basket. Fry for approximately 5 minutes or until the strips turn golden brown. Remove from fryer and place on paper towels to drain.

As the chicken is frying, take a small microwaveable bowl and mix in the butter and hot sauce. Pop it into the microwave for 25 seconds or until completely melted. (Use a small saucepan if you do not have a microwave)

Pour hot sauce mixture over the chicken strips and gently toss before serving.

Makes approximately 4 servings.

# Awesome Homemade Potato Chips

## Ingredients

4 medium potatoes, peeled and sliced paper-thin
3 tablespoons salt

## Directions

Slice the 4 potatoes as thin as you can get them. Use a knife, but you might also try using a potato peeler. It works well in producing thinner chips.

Place the potatoes in a large bowl of hot water. Let them soak for 20-25 minutes so that it removes most all of the starch from the potatoes.

While potatoes are soaking, heat oil in deep fryer to 370 degrees F.

Drain the potatoes and pat-dry before frying. Drop small batches of potatoes into deep fryer. Fry until they turn golden brown and remove. Place on paper towels to drain. Sprinkle with salt to taste before serving. Store uneaten chips in food storage bag.

Makes approximately 8 servings.

# Dill-icious Deep Fried Dill Pickles

## Ingredients

2 eggs
1 cup buttermilk
1 tablespoon Worcestershire sauce
1/2 teaspoon vinegar-based hot pepper sauce
3/4 teaspoon cayenne pepper
1/4 teaspoon seasoning salt
1/4 teaspoon garlic powder
1 cup cornmeal
2 1/4 cups all-purpose flour
1 teaspoon salt
3/4 teaspoon ground black pepper
1 (32 oz.) jar dill pickle slices
salt and pepper to taste

## Directions

Heat oil in deep fryer to 365 degrees F.

Mix together the eggs, 1/4 cup of flour, buttermilk, hot sauce, Worcestershire sauce, cayenne pepper, salt and garlic powder in a large bowl and stir until well combined.

Next, use a separate bowl to add the cornmeal, remainder of flour, black pepper and salt. Quickly stir until mixed together.

Remove the dill pickles from jar to drain. Take each one and put it in the large liquid bowl. Then, dip it into the flour bowl and coat thoroughly.

Add pickles to deep fryer and fry until you see them turning a nice golden brown color. Remove from fryer and place on paper towels. Season with salt and pepper if desired and serve.

Makes approximately 12 servings.

# Fried Onion Volcano With Dipping Sauce

## Ingredients

## Dipping Sauce Ingredients

1/2 cup mayonnaise
1 tablespoon ketchup
2 tablespoons cream-style horseradish sauce
1/3 teaspoon paprika
1/4 teaspoon salt
1/8 teaspoon dried oregano
1 pinch ground black pepper
1/3 teaspoon cayenne pepper

## Blooming Onion Ingredients

1 egg
1 cup milk
1 cup all-purpose flour
1 1/2 teaspoons salt
1 1/2 teaspoons cayenne pepper
1 teaspoon paprika
1/2 teaspoon ground black pepper
1/3 teaspoon dried oregano
1/8 teaspoon dried thyme
1/8 teaspoon ground cumin
1 large sweet onion

## Directions

Dipping Sauce

In a small bowl, add all of the sauce ingredients and stir them until well combined. Cover the bowl and put it in the refrigerator for use later.

## Onion Batter

Use 2 separate medium sized bowls for this part of the recipe. In one bowl, beat in the egg and then add the milk, stirring until thoroughly mixed.

In the other bowl, add the salt, flour, paprika, cayenne pepper, black pepper, thyme, oregano and cumin. Stir until they become well combined.

Heat oil in deep fryer to 350 degrees F.

Next, slice the onion by taking approximately one-inch off the top and bottom with a knife. Remove excess skin. Then, use a smaller paring type of knife to remove the center core of the onion. You want to remove about a one-inch diameter center core.

Use a larger knife to make several cuts down the center of the onion, finishing three quarters of the way down. Continue to slice onion all the way around. Then do it a second time by slicing in an X across the sections you sliced earlier. Take your time as it can be a bit tricky.

Boil a small pot of water and place the onion in the water for one-minute in order to keep the "blossoms" spread apart. Immediately remove from boiling water and place in a bowl of cold water.

Remove the onion and allow excess water to drain before dipping it into the milk bowl. Take it out once covered and put the onion into the flour bow. You want to make sure you work the flour into all of the blossom areas so that everything is well coated.

Do a double-dip by repeating the process once again.

Add onion to deep fryer basket and fry for approximately 9-10 or until you see the onion turn brown. Remove from fryer and let excess oil drain by placing paper towels underneath of it.

Serve onion with dipping sauce. Makes approximately 6 servings.

# Easy Fried Crab Fritters

## Ingredients

3/4 cup light mayonnaise
1 tablespoon Dijon mustard
1 tablespoon prepared horseradish
2 cloves garlic, peeled
2 tablespoons fresh lemon juice
1 tablespoon chopped fresh chives
1 cup hush puppy mix
1/2 cup milk
1 egg
1 pound cooked lump crabmeat

## Directions

Heat oil in deep fryer to 375 degrees F.

## Sauce Directions

In a medium sized bowl, (you can use a food processor if you have one) mix in the mayonnaise, horseradish, mustard, garlic and lemon juice. Stir until well blended. Sprinkle on the chives over the top and put bowl in refrigerator until ready to serve.

## Crab Directions

In a medium bowl, combine the hush puppy mix with the egg and milk. Stir continuously until the batter is smooth in texture. Add in the crap and mix it evenly in the batter.

Using a tablespoon, scoop out spoonfuls of crab mixture and fry in deep fryer for 2-3 minutes or until they turn golden brown. Remove from fryer and place on paper towels to drain excess oil.

Take the sauce out of the refrigerator and serve with fritters.

Makes approximately 5 servings.

# Green Bay Fried Cheese Curds

## Ingredients

1/4 cup milk
1 cup all-purpose flour
3/4 cup beer
1/2 teaspoon salt
2 eggs
2 pounds cheese curds, broken apart

## Directions

Heat oil in deep fryer to 375 degrees F.

In a large bowl, stir in the flour, milk, beer, eggs and salt. Mix until well combined and smooth.

Add in 8 cheese curds at one time to the bowl and coat well. Place the curds in deep fryer for 2 minutes or until they turn golden brown. Remove from fryer and place on paper towels to drain. Serve immediately.

Makes approximately 16 servings.

# Deep Fried Mexican Jalapeno Slices

## Ingredients

    1 cup all-purpose flour
    1 teaspoon salt
    1 teaspoon black pepper
    1 teaspoon red chili powder
    1 teaspoon garlic powder
    2 eggs
    1 cup beer
    2 cups sliced jalapeno peppers

## Directions

Heat oil in deep fryer to 370 degrees F.

In a large bowl, add in the flour, pepper, salt, garlic powder, eggs, chili pepper and beer. Stir until well mixed with wooden spoon.

Take jalapeno slices and dip them into the batter. (TIP: Always wear gloves when handling jalapeno peppers to avoid skin irritation and burning) Let excess batter drip off before placing them into deep fryer.

Fry small batches for 1-2 minutes or until they are golden brown. Remove from oil and place on paper towels to drain.

Serve immediately. You can use a Ranch dressing for a dipping sauce, or even place the slices on a side of nachos.

Makes approximately 4-6 servings.

# Mamma's Onion Rings

## Ingredients

3 onions
2 1/2 cups buttermilk
1/2 teaspoon cayenne pepper
8 oz. plain flour
1 teaspoon celery salt
1/4 teaspoon garlic powder
1 teaspoon paprika

## Directions

Peel and cut onions into 1/4 or 1/2 inch slices. Separate the slices into individual onion rings.

In a large bowl, mix together the buttermilk and cayenne pepper. Add the onion rings and let soak for 45-60 minutes.

Heat oil in deep fryer to 375 degrees F.

In a separate medium bowl, combine the flour, garlic powder, paprika and celery salt and stir until well mixed.

Drain the large bowl of onion rings and put them into the flour mixture, coating well.

Put 4-5 rings in deep fryer and fry until they become golden brown and crispy. Remove from fryer and drain on paper towels. Add a little salt for seasoning and serve while hot.

Makes approximately 35 onion rings.

# Thai Style Beef Rolls

## Ingredients

### Beef Roll Ingredients

50 spring roll wrappers
1/2 lb. ground beef
5 large eggs
5 scallions, stalks finely chopped
2 teaspoons salt
2 teaspoons ground coriander

### Dipping Sauce Ingredients

1 cucumber, diced
1 large carrot, diced
5 Thai chilies, finely chopped
5 shallots, thinly sliced
3 tablespoons white vinegar
1 teaspoon granulated sugar
1/4 cup water

## Directions

### Dipping Sauce Directions

Add all sauce ingredients to blender and blend well. Pour in serving bowl and let chill in refrigerator for 45-60 minutes.

### Beef Roll Direction

Heat oil in deep fryer to 370 degrees F.

While oil is heating, brown the ground beef in a skillet over medium heat. Drain off the grease and put in a medium sized bowl.

Add in the salt, scallions, eggs and coriander to the bowl and mix together well.

In a spring roll wrapper, add a couple of tablespoons of beef mixture. (You may want to add a bit more if desired.) Fold sides of wrapper to create a rectangle shape.

Place 2-3 rolls in deep fryer and fry of 2-3 minutes before turning over. Remove when they turn golden brown and place on paper towels.

Serve with dipping sauce. Makes approximately 8 servings.

# Southwest Fried Cheese Balls

## Ingredients

1/2 lb. cheddar cheese, grated
6 ounces shrimp, peeled and chopped
1 1/2 tablespoons cilantro, chopped
1 tablespoon jalapeno chilies, seeded and chopped (canned or fresh)
1 pinch chili powder
1 cup flour
1/2 cup cornstarch
3/4 teaspoon baking powder
1 pinch salt
1 cup water
2 tablespoons vegetable oil
1 1/2 cup breadcrumbs

## Directions

Heat oil in deep fryer to 360 degrees F.

Add in the shrimp, cheese, chilies, cilantro and chili powder in a large bowl and mix well. Once mixed, make the mixture into 3/4 inch balls.

In a shallow dish, mix together the flour, cornstarch, salt and baking soda. Stir just until combined. Next, add water and 2 tablespoons oil and use a whisk to stir it all together.

On a separate plate, pour out the breadcrumbs.

Take the cheese balls and first place them in the batter dish. Next, roll them in the breadcrumbs.

Add them in the deep fryer and fry for 1-2 minutes or until you see them becoming golden brown. Remove from fryer and place on paper towels before serving.

Makes approximately 6 servings.

# Cindy's Fried Sweet Potato Balls

## Ingredients

3/4 pound sweet potatoes, cooked, peeled and mashed
4 teaspoons cornstarch, divided use
1 pinch salt
1 tablespoon water
1 cup shredded coconut
1/2 cup brown sugar
3/4 cup sesame seeds

## Directions

Heat oil in deep fryer to 375 degrees F.

Add sweet potatoes, 2 teaspoons cornstarch, salt and the water to a large bowl. Stir slowly and steadily until you find the mixture turning into a dough.

In another medium bowl, mix together the coconut and brown sugar, stirring until well combined.

Take the potato dough and shape it into 1-2 inch balls. Next, use your finger to put a depression in the center of each ball and add the coconut mixture to it. Re-form the balls and run them through the sesame seeds and corn starch.

Add 5-6 balls to deep fryer and fry until they become golden brown. Remove from oil and place on paper towels to drain before serving.

Makes approximately 5 servings.

# Not Just For Kids Macaroni and Cheese Balls

## Ingredients

4 quarts water
1 teaspoon salt, divided
2 cups uncooked elbow macaroni
1/2 cup milk
3 tablespoons milk
1 (12 oz.) package cheese spread, cubed
1 cup mozzarella cheese, shredded
1/4 teaspoon ground black pepper
4 large eggs
2 cups Italian seasoned breadcrumbs
1/2 cup yellow cornmeal

## Directions

Take a 13x9 baking dish and lightly grease the bottom before setting aside on counter for later.

In a large saucepan, bring to boiling on high, 3 quarts of water and 1/2 teaspoon of salt. Mix in the macaroni and cook for 7 minutes, stirring occasionally. Remove and drain water.

Immediately put the cooked macaroni in a large bowl along with the half cup of milk, mozzarella cheese, salt, pepper and cheese spread. Stir continuously until cheeses melt. Add the entire contents of bowl into the baking dish. Cover with plastic wrap and place in refrigerator for approximately 8 hours.

Next, take the dish out of the refrigerator and use your fingers to roll the macaroni into one-inch balls. Put all of the balls onto a cookie sheet and place in freezer for 1-2 hours.

Heat oil in deep fryer to 350 degrees F.

Get out two small bowls and add the eggs and remaining milk in one of them. Stir until well mixed. In the second bowl, add the cornmeal and breadcrumbs. Mix together until combined.

Take macaroni balls out of freezer and dip each one first into the milk mixture and then into the breadcrumbs. Place 5-6 balls in deep fryer at one time for 3-4 minutes or until you see them become golden brown. Remove from fryer and place on paper towels before serving.

Makes approximately 60 balls.

# Hot & Spicy Fried Artichokes

## Ingredients

24 baby artichokes
2 quarts water
2 tablespoons lemon juice
2 eggs
1/2 cup Asian chili-garlic sauce
1/2 teaspoon onion powder
1 dash salt
1 dash cayenne pepper
Panko crumbs

## Directions

Heat oil in deep fryer to 375 degrees F.

Run artichokes through cold water to clean. Next, add the lemon juice and 2 quarts water to a large bowl.

Trim the artichokes by removing the stems and top thirds of the petals. Use your fingers or just your thumb to bend back 3-4 petals at one time until they break off. Work your way around the artichoke to break off all the petals. The goal is to have only dull yellow leaves left. Cut each artichoke into 4 pieces.

Add the eggs to a medium bowl and beat them in well. Then, add the garlic sauce, cayenne, onion powder and salt. Mix until well combined.

In another plate or pie pan, place the breadcrumbs in it. Put an artichoke in the egg bowl and coat. Next, run it through the breadcrumbs before placing them in the deep fryer.

Fry 3-4 artichokes at a time for approximately 2-3 minutes or until you see them becoming brown. Remove from fryer and place on paper towels before serving.

Makes approximately 6 servings.

# Cheesy Sweet Potato Chips

## Ingredients

> 5 lbs. sweet potatoes
> coarse salt
> black pepper (optional)
> 3 cups shredded mozzarella cheese

## Directions

Heat oil in deep fryer to 375 degrees F.

Slice sweet potatoes into very thin slices using a knife or potato peeler. Remove excess water from the chips by patting them with paper towels.

Add potatoes to deep fryer in small batches and fry for 1-2 minutes or until you see them turning golden brown. Remove from fryer and place on paper towels.

Next, heat oven to broil and place chips on a cookie or baking sheet. Sprinkle with some salt and pepper, along with adding the shredded cheese over the top. Place in broiler for 3-4 minutes or until you see that the cheese has thoroughly melted over the chips.

Remove from broiler and put on serving tray. Makes approximately 6 servings.

# Midwest Style Fried Tortellini's

## Ingredients

1 (16 oz.) package refrigerated or fresh cheese tortellini
1/2 cup bread crumbs
1/2 cup cornflake crumbs
salt and pepper to taste
dried parsley, to taste
3 eggs, lightly beaten

## Directions

Prepare the package of tortellini as stated on the package directions. Once cooked, soak in ice cold water for a couple of minutes until they cool off.

Heat oil in deep fryer to 360 degrees F.

Get a one-gallon storage bag and add in the breadcrumbs, cornflake crumbs, parsley, salt and pepper. Shake to combine.

In a small bowl, beat in the eggs. Next, take the tortellini's and dip in egg bowl and then add to the breadcrumb bag. Give the bag a shake and be sure tortellinis are well covered.

Deep fry small amounts until they become golden brown in fryer. Remove and place on paper towels to drain. Serve warm with tomato sauce if desired.

Makes approximately 6 servings.

# Southern Style Black Eyed Peas

## Ingredients

1 pound dried black-eyed peas, sorted and rinsed
1 onion, cut into large dice
2 bay leaves
1 jalapeno pepper, seeded and diced
2 teaspoons seafood seasoning
1/2 teaspoon kosher salt

## Directions

In a large bowl with a lid, add the black eyed peas and fill with cold water. Let the bowl sit on the counter overnight.

Remove the peas from the bowl and rinse them off. Put them into a large saucepan and fill saucepan with water. Add in the onion, bay leaves and jalapeno pepper and heat to boiling.

Turn the heat down to low and let the peas simmer for 45 minutes. You want the peas to become tender. If the water level becomes too low in the saucepan, add a little more.

Heat oil in deep fryer to 375 degrees F.

Pour out the peas into a strainer to drain. Next, place paper towels on a baking or cookie sheet and add the peas over the top to drain excess water. Toss out the bay leaves.

Place one cup of peas in deep fryer at a time and fry for 5-6 minutes. Remove from fryer and put them on paper towels to drain before adding them to a serving dish. You can season with salt or your favorite seafood seasoning.

Makes approximately 16 servings.

# Old Fashioned Deep Fried Chicken Wings

## Ingredients

12 chicken wings, first and second parts, divided, defrosted
2 tablespoons garfava bean flour
1/3 cup cornstarch
1/3 cup tapioca starch
1/4 cup sorghum flour
4 tablespoons dry rub seasonings
1 egg
1/3 cup milk

## Directions

Heat oil in deep fryer to 375 degrees F.

Preheat oven to 250 degrees F.

In a medium sized bowl that also has a lid, mix in both flours, both starches and the dry rub seasoning. Put the lid on and shake for a few seconds.

In a small bowl, mix the egg and milk together, stirring well.

Take several chicken wings and put in flour bowl to coat. Then, run them through the egg bowl. Finally, put them back in the flour bowl and shake again. Put the prepared chicken on a plate or baking sheet.

Deep fry 5-6 wings in fryer at one time for 10 minutes or until you see them turn golden brown and crispy. Remove from fryer and place on paper towels. While waiting on other batches to deep fry, place the cooked wings in preheated oven to stay warm.

Serve wings with your favorite dipping sauce.

Makes approximately 4 servings.

# Deep Sea Crabmeat Balls

## Ingredients

1 cup fine dry breadcrumbs
6 1/2 oz. crabmeat
1/2 cup milk
2 tablespoons all-purpose flour
1 tablespoon butter
2 beaten eggs
1/2 teaspoon onion, minced
1/2 teaspoon finely chopped parsley
1/2 teaspoon mustard
1/2 teaspoon Worcestershire sauce
1 teaspoon salt
1 dash pepper

## Directions

In a large saucepan, add butter and melt on med-low heat. Next, add the four and milk, stir constantly until the mixture thickens.

Take the crabmeat and cut it into small pieces and add it to the saucepan. Also mix in the Worcestershire sauce, onion, parsley, salt and pepper. Stir until well combined and remove from heat.

Take the crab mixture and put inside a pan and place it in the refrigerator for 30 minutes to quickly chill.

Heat oil in deep fryer to 360 degrees F.

Remove crab mixture from refrigerator and form it into individual balls about one-inch in diameter. Add the breadcrumbs to a plate or small pan. Also beat in the eggs in a small bowl.

Roll the balls in the breadcrumbs. Then roll them in the egg bowl, and finally, back through the breadcrumbs. Fry small batches in deep fryer until you see them become golden brown in color. Remove from fryer and place on paper towels to drain before serving.

Makes approximately 25 balls.

# Deep Fried Ham Balls

## Ingredients

1 lb. cooked ham, ground or very finely chopped
1 1/2 lbs. lean bulk pork sausage
1/4 cup finely chopped onion
2 tablespoons very finely chopped green bell pepper
2 cups fine dry bread crumbs
2 eggs, beaten
1/2 cup milk
1 tablespoon brown sugar, packed
1 teaspoon dry mustard

## Directions

Heat oil in deep fryer to 365 degrees F.

Take all of the ingredients and add them to a large bowl and mix them together until they are thoroughly combined.

Using your hands, form one-inch balls out of the mixture.

Add ham balls to deep fryer in small batches of 6-8 each. Fry for 3-4 minutes or until they become golden brown and crisp. Remove from fryer and place on paper towels to drain excess oil.

The ham balls can be served alone or with any of your favorite dipping sauces.

Makes approximately 12 servings.

# Mexican Party Appetizers

## Ingredients

1 lb. ground beef
1 medium onion, chopped
Salt and pepper
1 can refried beans
1-1/2 cups shredded cheddar cheese
1 cup salsa
1 can (4 oz.) diced jalapeno peppers, drained
2 packages (12 oz. each) wonton wrappers
Salsa for dipping

## Directions

Heat oil in deep fryer to 375 degrees F.

Add the hamburger, onion, salt and pepper to a large skillet on medium heat, stirring regularly until the beef is browned.

Drain excess oil from the beef before adding in the beans, jalapenos, cheese and salsa. Turn the heat down to low and cook the mixture just until you see the cheese melt. Remove the skillet from the heat and allow to cool for approximately 8-10 minutes.

Lay out a wonton wrapper and scoop out a heaping teaspoonful of beef and place in the middle of the wrapper. Moisten the wrapper and fold one corner up to the opposite corner on the other end to form a triangle. Continue the process with the rest of the beef.

Add small batches of beef wontons to deep fryer and fry for 3 minutes or until you the wrappers becoming golden brown. Remove from fryer and place on paper towels to drain before serving. Use your favorite salsa for dipping.

Makes approximately 24 servings.

# Down Home Sweet Calas

## Ingredients

    1 pkg. active dry yeast
    1/2 cup warm water
    1 1/2 cups cooked short grain rice
    3 eggs, beaten
    1/4 cup sugar
    1 1/4 cups all-purpose flour
    1/2 teaspoon salt
    1/4 teaspoon ground nutmeg
    1/2 cups powdered sugar
    1 tablespoon ground cinnamon

## Directions

In a medium bowl, add the yeast and water. Next, mash up the cooked rice by using a potato masher or the back of a tablespoon. Let the rice cool down before mixing it into the yeast bowl. Stir it in well and then put a lid over the bowl and let it sit out overnight in an area that is warm. You want the yeast to be able to rise.

Heat oil in deep fryer to 375 degrees F.

Open up the bowl the following morning and combine the eggs, flour, sugar, nutmeg and salt into the mixture and stir it together well.

Using a spoon, drop spoonfuls of the mixture in small batches into deep fryer. Fry until you see them become golden brown. Remove and place on paper towels.

Take the cinnamon and powdered sugar and add it over the top of the calas to taste.

Makes approximately 12 servings.

# All American Beer Battered Onion Rings

## Ingredients

1 1/3 cup all-purpose flour
1 teaspoon salt
2 large sweet onions, sliced
1/4 teaspoon pepper
1 tablespoon vegetable oil
2 egg yolks
3/4 cup beer

## Directions

Heat oil in deep fryer to 375 degrees F.

On a cutting board, slice onions in 1/4 inch slices. Separate each slice into individual rings.

In a large bowl, combine the flour, egg, oil, salt and pepper. Stir ingredients until they are thoroughly mixed and you have a smooth batter.

Dip onion rings in batter and drop small batches in deep fryer for 1-2 minutes or until they turn golden brown. Remove from fryer and place on paper towels to drain. Season with salt if desired before serving.

Makes approximately 8 servings.

# Top Shelf Seasoned French Fries

## Ingredients

  2 1/2 lbs. russet potatoes, peeled
  1 cup all-purpose flour
  1 teaspoon paprika
  1 teaspoon onion salt
  1 teaspoon garlic salt
  1 teaspoon salt
  1/2 cup water, or as needed

## Directions

Heat oil in deep fryer to 375 degrees F.

Slice the potatoes into 3-4 inch long French fries. Add them to a large bowl of cold water and set aside.

In a separate large bowl, combine the flour, paprika and all 3 salts. Next, slowly begin adding the water and stir continuously. Add only enough water to where the batter has a thick consistency.

Add small amounts of French fries to the batter and cover completely. Place in deep fryer one at a time so they do not stick together. Fry until they become golden brown. Remove from fryer and place on paper towels to drain excess oil before serving.

Makes approximately 8 servings.

# Grandma's Deep Fried Spinach Balls

## Ingredients

2 cups chopped cooked spinach
2 tablespoons butter
2 tablespoons grated onions
2 tablespoons grated cheese
Salt and pepper
2 eggs, divided
1 cup bread crumbs
1/8 teaspoon allspice
1/4 cup water
1 cup fine dry bread crumbs

## Directions

Heat oil in deep fryer to 365 degrees F.

In a large bowl, mix together one of the eggs, butter, salt, pepper, spinach, onion, cheese, allspice and breadcrumbs. Stir until thoroughly mixed and let it sit for 8-10 minutes.

Use a spoon to form scoop mixture into one-inch diameter balls.

In a separate bowl, beat in the other egg and add the 1/4 cup of water. Stir till combined. Add the breadcrumbs to another small bowl as well.

Next, roll each one of the spinach balls through the breadcrumb bowl, then into the egg bowl, and finally, once again through the breadcrumbs.

Add 4-5 balls at a time to deep fryer and fry for 1-2 minutes or until they turn a nice golden brown color. Remove from fryer and place on paper towels to drain before serving.

Makes approximately 6 servings.

# Deep Fried Shrimp Fritters

## Ingredients

3 tablespoons butter
1 lb. medium sized shrimp, peeled and deveined
4 green onions, finely chopped (include tops)
1 bell pepper, seeded and finely chopped
1 small hot or mild chile pepper, seeded and finely chopped
2 cups mashed potatoes
2 eggs, beaten
salt and pepper, to taste
1 cup fine dry bread crumbs

## Directions

In a large skillet, add the butter to medium heat and melt. Next, mix in the shrimp and stir occasionally for 3 minutes or until you see them turning pink. Take the shrimp out of the skillet and place on cutting board to cool before chopping them up.

In the same skillet with the butter, add in the bell pepper, onions and the chile pepper and stir over medium heat for 3 minutes.

Combine the skillet ingredients into the mashed potatoes and mix together thoroughly. Next, mix in the eggs and shrimp before seasoning with salt and pepper. Stir until combined.

Roll the mixture into 1-2 inch balls. Put the breadcrumbs in a pie pan and roll the shrimp balls in the breadcrumbs. Once you have made all the shrimp balls, put them in a bowl with a lid and place in refrigerator for 2-3 hours.

Heat oil in deep fryer to 365 degrees F.

Add 4-5 shrimp balls to deep fryer and fry for 3-1/2 minutes or until the outside becomes lightly brown and crispy. Remove from fryer and place on paper towels to drain before serving.

Makes approximately 8 servings.

# Blue Cheese Style Buffalo Wings

## Chicken Ingredients

4 lbs. chicken wings
Salt and pepper
1/4 cup butter
1/4 cup hot pepper sauce
1 tablespoon white vinegar

## Blue Cheese Dip Ingredients

3/4 cup mayonnaise
1 clove garlic, minced
2 tablespoons finely chopped fresh parsley
1/2 cup sour cream
1 tablespoon fresh lemon juice
1 tablespoon white vinegar
1/2 cup crumbled blue cheese
salt and pepper

## Blue Cheese Dip Directions

Add all of the ingredients into a medium sized bowl and mix them until well combined. Place some plastic wrap over the top of the bowl and chill in the refrigerator for 60 minutes.

## Chicken Wing Directions

Heat oil in deep fryer to 370 degrees F.

Add salt and pepper to the chicken wings before frying in deep fryer. Fry small batches of 6-8 wings for 10 minutes or until nicely browned and crisp on the outside. Remove from fryer and place on paper towels. Cover and keep warm as you fry up the rest of the wings.

Next, melt the butter in a small pan and add in the vinegar and hot sauce. Stir quickly before pouring the sauce on top of the wings. Serve hot wings with the blue cheese dip.

Makes approximately 24 servings.

# Delicious Fried Pizza Sticks

## Ingredients

    1 (14 oz.) package egg roll wrappers
    24 (1 oz.) pieces string cheese
    25 (4 oz.) packages sliced pepperoni sausage, cut into strips
    1 (6 oz.) can sliced mushrooms, drained
    2 tablespoons minced garlic
    1 (14 oz.) jar of tomato and basil sauce

## Directions

Heat oil in deep fryer to 370 degrees F.

Take an egg roll wrapper, flatten it out and add a piece of string cheese in the middle. Lay a few pepperonis and mushrooms, as well as some garlic, in the wrapper. Fold to form into pizza sticks by rolling up a little of the string cheese, then folding in the sides of the wrapper. Complete by rolling the wrapper the rest of the way up and sealing off the edges.

Add 2-3 sticks to deep fryer and fry for 7-8 minutes or until you see them turning brown. Turn once at the halfway mark. Remove from fryer and place on paper towels.

While frying pizza sticks, add the tomato sauce to a medium pan and heat on low.

Plate the pizza sticks and add sauce to serving bowl.

Makes approximately 24 servings.

# Spicy Jalapeno Poppers

## Ingredients

15 jalapeno peppers
8 oz. cream cheese, softened
1/2 cup shredded Cheddar cheese
1 cup milk
1 cup all-purpose flour
Pinch of salt
1 cup plain dry breadcrumbs

## Directions

Prepare the jalapenos by cutting them apart lengthwise and removing all of the seeds. (TIP: I would always advise wearing gloves when working with jalapeno peppers to avoid skin irritation.)

In a small bowl, mix together the softened cream cheese and the cheddar cheese. Stir until it is mixed together thoroughly.

Spread the cheese mixture inside each jalapeno pepper before putting them back together again.

Pour out the milk in a small bowl. In another small bowl, add in the flour and salt and quickly stir together. Finally, add the breadcrumbs in a third bowl.

Heat oil in deep fryer to 375 degrees F.

Take each pepper half and dip it first in milk, then next it goes in the breadcrumb bowl. Allow the pepper to then dry for 8-10 minutes.

Add 4-5 pepper halves to deep fryer at one time and fry for approximately 3 minutes or until you see the peppers becoming nicely browned. Remove from fryer and drain on paper towels before serving.

Makes approximately 6 servings.

# Fried Mozzarella Cheese Squares

## Ingredients

1 lb. Mozzarella cheese, cut into sticks or cubes
2/3 cup all-purpose flour
3 large eggs, beaten
3/4 cup Italian seasoned bread crumbs

## Directions

Heat oil in deep fryer to 365 degrees F.

Take 3 small bowls or pie pans and fill one with flour, one with the breadcrumbs and the third with the beaten eggs.

Cut the mozzarella cheese into small sticks or cubes, or a combination of both if you desire.

Take each cheese stick and put it in the flour bowl, then the egg bowl, and finally through the breadcrumb bowl.

Add small batches of cheese sticks to deep fryer and fry for approximately 3 minutes or until you see them turn golden brown. Remove from fryer and drain on paper towels before serving.

Makes approximately 24 servings.

# Country Fried Mushrooms

## Ingredients

1 pound morel mushrooms
2 eggs
3/4 cup milk
1 (4 oz.) packet saltine crackers, finely crushed
Salt and pepper

## Directions

Heat oil in deep fryer to 360 degrees F.

Prepare the mushrooms by rinsing and cleaning them with paper towels or a soft brush. Slice them into smaller bite-size pieces if they are too large.

In a medium bowl, beat in the two eggs and pour in the milk. Stir until well combined. In a second bowl, add in the breadcrumbs.

Put each mushroom into the egg bowl first, and then transfer to the breadcrumb bowl. Be sure each is coated well.

Add to deep fryer and fry for 1-2 minutes or until you see them turn golden brown. Turn them over and fry on other side for 1 minute. Remove from fryer and place on paper towels.

Add salt and pepper to taste before serving.

Makes approximately 4 servings.

# Nancy's Italian Style Deep Fried Zucchini

## Ingredients

24 zucchini blossoms
3⁄4 lb. mozzarella
12 anchovy filets
4 eggs
1 cup flour
Salt and ground black pepper

## Directions

Heat oil in deep fryer to 400 degrees F.

Prepare the zucchini blossoms by cutting off the stems and stamens and rinsing them. Dry carefully with paper towels.

Take the mozzarella and slice it into small cubes. Do the same with the anchovy fillets before combining both of them to a medium bowl.

Take a blossom and stuff the mixture inside it. Then, twist the petals so that the mixture stays inside the blossom. Repeat for remaining blossoms.

In another medium bowl, mix in the 4 eggs until well combined. In a third bowl, mix together the flour along with the salt and pepper.

Dip the blossoms first into the flour, coating well. Then run them through the egg bowl before adding them back into the flour bowl.

Add a small batch to deep fryer and fry for 5 minutes or until they become nicely browned and crisp. Remove from fryer and place on paper towels. Season with salt and pepper to taste.

Makes approximately 6-8 servings.

# Picadillo Deep Fried Potato Croquettes

## Ingredients

2 lbs. potatoes, peeled and quartered
Salt
3 eggs, separated
Pinch nutmeg
1/4 cup minced fresh parsley
1 cup Picadillo
1 cup bread crumbs

## Directions

Add potatoes and a bit of salt to a pot of cold water and cook on medium heat for 30 minutes. After potatoes are cooked, drain the water out and mash so that they become smooth. Leave them for 20 minutes to cool.

Heat oil in deep fryer to 360 degrees F.

In two small bowls, separate the egg yolks and whites. In the bowl with the yolks, add in the parsley and nutmeg. Stir until combined, adding a pinch of salt to taste as well.

In the bowl with the egg whites, simply whisk or stir until well mixed. At the same time, add the breadcrumbs to a separate bowl.

Using your hands, form the potato mixture into 1-inch balls. Use your finger to create a well in the middle of the ball and place a tablespoon of picadillo in it. Re-form the ball with the picadillo in the middle.

Take each filled ball and put it in the egg white bowl, then transfer it over to the breadcrumb bowl.

Place balls in small batches in the deep fryer. Fry for 4 minutes or until you see the balls become golden brown. Remove from fryer and set on paper towels to drain.

Makes approximately 6 servings.

# Deep Fried San Francisco Scallions

## Ingredients

> 1 cup white wine
> 1 cup flour
> Salt and ground black pepper
> 4 bunches of thin scallions, trimmed

## Directions

Heat oil in deep fryer to 360 degrees F.

In a medium bowl, add the white wine and flour. Mix until it becomes nice and smooth.

Slice scallions in half crosswise. Next, coat them in the bowl with the batter.

Drop in deep fryer and fry for 3 minutes or until they are nicely browned. Remove from fryer and set on paper towels to drain excess oil.

Season with salt and pepper to taste and serve.

Makes approximately 4 servings.

# Ocean Fresh Prawn Balls

## Ingredients

1 slice white bread (fairly thick crusts removed)
2 tablespoons chicken broth (stock)
1 lb. shrimp (raw, peeled headless very finely chopped 500g)
4 water chestnuts (finely chopped from a tin)
1 teaspoon fresh ginger (finely grated)
1 pinch salt (seasoning, choice but remember broth can be salty)
3-4 drops hot sauce
1 egg yolk
1 egg white (beaten)

## Directions

Heat oil in deep fryer to 375 degrees F.

In a small bowl, add the sliced bread and chicken stock. (The bread is supposed to absorb the chicken stock.) Remove the bread carefully and place in another large bowl.

Combine the shrimp, water chestnuts, ginger, egg yolk, salt and hot sauce in the large bowl with the bread. Stir until well mixed. Next, add the egg white and continue stirring.

Use your hands to form mixture into 1-2 inch diameter balls.

Add small batches of balls into deep fryer and fry for approximately 2 minutes or until they become golden brown. Remove from fryer and drain on paper towels before serving.

Makes approximately 4 servings.

# Deep Fried Tofu

## Ingredients

    1 lb. medium or firm tofu
    3 - 4 tablespoons cornstarch or flour

## Directions

Heat oil in fryer to 350 degrees F.

Prepare tofu by draining and then slicing into four distinct squares.

Add the cornstarch or flour, (whichever you prefer) on waxed paper or flat work station. Next, roll and cover the tofu with the flour or cornstarch thoroughly.

Drop tofu into deep fryer and fry until each side becomes golden brown. Remove from fryer and place on paper towels to drain before serving.

Makes approximately 4 servings.

# Teriyaki Style Chicken Wings

## Ingredients

3 lbs.
1 cup all-purpose flour
1-1/2 teaspoons garlic powder
1 teaspoon salt
1/2 teaspoon pepper
3/4 cup soy sauce
3/4 cup sugar

## Directions

Heat oil in deep fryer to 360 degrees F.

Prepare chicken wings by slicing them into 3 pieces and getting rid of the tips.

Mix together the flour, salt, pepper and garlic in a one-gallon food storage bag. Place the wings inside and toss for 10 seconds or until they are thoroughly coated.

Place small batches of wings in deep fryer and fry for 8-9 minutes or until they become golden brown and crispy. Remove from fryer and put them on paper towels to drain excess oil.

While the chicken wings are frying, mix the sugar and soy sauce in a medium saucepan. Heat on low-med and stir for 4-5 minutes or until the sugar completely dissolves.

Add the cooked wings into the sauce and remove to a serving plate.

Makes approximately 12 servings.

# John's Classic Corn Balls

## Ingredients

1 cup all-purpose flour
1-1/2 teaspoons baking powder
2 eggs, beaten
1/3 cup milk
1 can (15-1/4 oz.) whole kernel corn, drained
1 tablespoon butter, melted
1 tablespoon honey
Confectioners' sugar
Maple syrup

## Directions

Heat oil in deep fryer to 375 degrees F.

Mix together the flour and baking powder in a large size bowl. Next, add in the beaten eggs and gradually pour in the milk, stirring until well combined. Finally, mix in the butter and corn and lightly stir until mixed.

Use a teaspoon to scoop out spoonfuls and form into 1-inch diameter balls. Drop the balls in small batches into deep fryer and fry for 3 minutes or until the balls turn golden brown in color.

Remove from fryer and place on paper towels to drain excess oil. Sprinkle confectioner's sugar over the balls and serve with warm maple syrup. The taste is incredible.

Makes approximately 6 servings.

# Spicy Southwest Onion Rings

## Ingredients

2 large sweet Vidalia onions
2-1/2 cups buttermilk
2 eggs
3 tablespoons water
1-3/4 cups all-purpose flour
2 teaspoons salt
2 teaspoons chili powder
1 or 2 teaspoons cayenne pepper
1 teaspoon sugar
1 teaspoon garlic powder
1 teaspoon ground cumin

## Directions

Remove dead skin from onions before slicing them into 1/4 to 1/2 inch slices. Take each slice and separate them into individual onion rings. Add the rings and the buttermilk to a large bowl and stir together. Cover the bowl with a lid or plastic wrap for 25-30 minutes.

Heat oil in deep fryer to 380 degrees F.

Get 2 pie pans or large bowls and add the eggs and water to one of them. Stir until well mixed. In the second bowl, mix together the flour, chili powder, salt, garlic powder, cayenne pepper, cumin and sugar. Stir until combined.

Take the onion rings out of the buttermilk and let drain. Next, place each ring into the egg bowl and then into the flour bowl. Be sure they are well coated. You can double-dip them as well if you prefer.

Add small batches of rings to deep fryer and fry for 1-2 minutes per side, or until you see them become golden brown. Do not overcook. Remove from fryer and place on paper towels to drain.

Makes approximately 8 servings.

# Sweet Honey Butter Puffs

## Ingredients

1/4 cup plus 3 tablespoons butter, softened, divided use
1/4 cup honey
3 eggs
1 cup (8 oz.) plain yogurt
2 cups all-purpose flour
2 teaspoons baking powder
1 teaspoon baking soda
1/2 teaspoon ground nutmeg
1/4 teaspoon salt

## Directions

Heat oil in deep fryer to 365 degrees F.

Get out 2 large bowls and add the honey and 1/4 cup of butter to the first one. Stir it until the mixture becomes smooth and well combined. This will be the honey butter for use later.

In the second bowl, beat the 3 eggs. Next, mix in the yogurt and 3 tablespoons of butter. Stir until this mixture becomes smooth as well. Then add the flour, baking soda, nutmeg, salt and baking powder, stirring constantly until thoroughly mixed.

Using a teaspoon, scoop rounded spoonfuls into deep fryer. Fry in batches of 6-8 for 2 minutes or until they turn golden brown, turning over at the one minute mark. Remove from fryer and place on paper towels to drain excess oil.

Add balls to serving plate along with honey butter.

Makes approximately 12 servings.

# Deep Fried Pork Rinds

## Ingredients

1/2 lb. pork rinds

## Directions

Heat oil in deep fryer to 370 degrees F.

Prepare the pork rinds by rinsing and cleaning, then cutting them into 2 inch pieces.

Drop small batches into deep fryer and fry for 3-4 minutes or until you see them turn golden brown. Remove from fryer and put on paper towels to drain excess oil before serving.

Makes approximately 6 servings.

# Deep Fried Zucchini And Carrot Fritters

## Sauce Ingredients

2/3 cup plus 1/2 cup sour cream, divided use
2/3 cup lightly packed fresh basil leaves
1 teaspoon lemon juice
Salt and pepper to taste
1/2 cup mayonnaise
1/2 cup horseradish sauce

## Fritter Ingredients

2 tablespoons finely chopped onion
1 tablespoon butter
1 egg, lightly beaten
2 medium zucchini, shredded and squeezed dry (about 1-1/2 cups)
1 large carrot, shredded
1/3 cup all-purpose flour
1/3 cup grated Parmesan cheese
1 tablespoon cornmeal
1/2 teaspoon salt
1/8 teaspoon pepper

## Directions

In a small bowl, mix together the 1/2 cup sour cream, mayonnaise and horseradish. Stir until well combined before putting a lid or plastic wrap over the bowl and setting in refrigerator.

Add the lemon juice, basil, 2/3 cup of sour cream, along with the salt and pepper in a blender. Blend until well combined and pour into another small bowl. Cover this bowl and refrigerate as well.

Heat oil in deep fryer to 375 degrees F.

In a microwavable container, add the onion and butter. Heat on high with a cover over the bowl until the onion becomes tender, usually about 45-60 seconds.

Take the bowl out of the microwave and mix in the zucchini, carrot and egg. In a separate small bowl, add in the cornmeal, flour, cheese and salt and pepper. Stir until mixed. Then, stir in the zucchini and carrot container and quickly mix together.

Use a teaspoon or tablespoon to scoop out mixture and add to deep fryer in small batches of 5-6 each. Fry for 3 minutes or until they turn golden brown. Turn over halfway through. Remove from fryer and place on paper towels before serving with the 2 sauces.

Makes approximately 8 servings.

# Italian Deep Fried Ravioli

## Ingredients

2 tablespoons parmesan cheese
1/2 teaspoon dried oregano leaves; crushed
1 Egg
2 cups spaghetti sauce
2 tablespoon water
14 oz. ravioli, thawed
1/2 cup fine dry bread crumbs

## Directions

Heat oil in deep fryer to 375 degrees F.

Mix the egg and water together in a small bowl and stir until well combined.

Add the oregano, parmesan cheese and breadcrumbs to a second small bowl and quickly stir together.

Take the thawed ravioli and first put them in the egg bowl, then add them to the breadcrumb bowl and coat each one well.

Drop small batches of ravioli in deep fryer for 2 minutes or until you see them becoming golden brown, turning them over halfway through. Remove from fryer and put them on paper towels to drain excess oil.

In a medium saucepan while ravioli is frying, add the spaghetti sauce and heat on low-med. Serve with raviolis.

Makes approximately 4 servings.

# Georgia Deep Fried Plantains

## Ingredients

3 cups water
3 green plantains, peeled
3 teaspoons salt
3 cloves garlic, chopped

## Directions

Heat oil in deep fryer to 375 degrees F.

Mix together the plantains, garlic, 2-3/4 teaspoon salt and water in a large bowl. Let the plantains sit for 12-15 minutes before removing from the water and drying off. (Save the water for later)

Drop the plantains in deep fryer and fry for approximately 6-7 minutes. Remove from fryer and place on paper towels to drain excess oil. (Do not turn fryer off)

Once the plantains have cooled to the point you can pick them up and handle, flatten them out to about 1/4 inch thick. You can use your palm or even a hardback book if you prefer.

Place the plantains back into the deep fryer and fry for another 2-3 minutes or until they become golden brown and crispy. Remove from oil and place on paper towels to drain off the excess oil again.

Season to taste with salt and serve.

Makes approximately 6 servings.

# Hot & Spicy Fried Onion Rings

## Ingredients

4 large Vidalia onions
1 cup egg substitute
1 cup all-purpose flour
2 cups bread crumbs
1 teaspoon salt
2 teaspoons ground black pepper
1 1/2 teaspoons cayenne pepper
1 teaspoon dried oregano
1 teaspoon dried basil
2 teaspoons red pepper flakes

## Directions

Heat oil in deep fryer to 375 degrees F.

Prepare onion rings by peeling and slicing each onion into 1/4 inch slices and separating into individual rings.

Get 3 medium bowls and add the flour to the first one. Then add the egg substitute to the second one, while adding the breadcrumbs, cayenne, oregano, basil, red pepper and salt and pepper to the third bowl.

Take each onion ring and place it in the flour bowl, then into the egg bowl, and finally into the breadcrumb bowl.

Drop small batches of rings into deep fryer for 1-2 minutes or until they turn golden brown. Turn them over halfway through. Remove from oil and drain on paper towels before serving. (Salt to taste)

Makes approximately 8 servings.

# Fried Sea Salt Peanuts

## Ingredients

Peanuts - shelled
Sea salt

## Directions

Heat oil in deep fryer to 375 degrees F.

This is a quick and simple recipe for an anytime snack.

Drop peanuts in fryer basket and down into deep fryer.

Fry in hot oil until the peanuts begin to turn brown. Remove and drain on paper towels. Sprinkle with sea salt to taste.

Store leftover peanuts in airtight plastic container.

# Dinners

# Flaming Hot Chicken Bites

## Ingredients

  3 lbs. boneless chicken breasts
  1/8 teaspoon salt
  1/8 teaspoon garlic powder
  2 tablespoons cayenne pepper
  1/2 teaspoon black pepper
  1 cup all-purpose flour

## Directions

Slice chicken breasts into 1 inch strips and season with salt, black pepper, cayenne pepper and garlic pepper. Place chicken strips in refrigerator for 45-60 minutes so seasonings will blend in their flavors.

Heat oil in deep fryer to 375 degrees F.

Add flour to a small bowl and dip strips into bowl. Drop small batches into deep fryer and fry for 2 minutes. Turn the chicken strips over and fry an additional 1-2 minutes. Remove from oil and place on paper towels to drain oil.

Serve chicken strips hot and with your favorite dipping sauces.

Makes approximately 8 servings.

# Hawaiian Pineapple Drumsticks

## Drumstick Ingredients

1 egg, slightly beaten
1/4 cup water
2 tablespoons milk
1/4 cup all-purpose flour
1 tablespoon cornstarch
1 tablespoon cornmeal
1/8 teaspoon baking powder
12 broiler-fryer chicken drumsticks

## Pineapple Sauce Ingredients

1 cup green pepper chunks
1/2 cup coarsely chopped onion
1 tablespoon Crisco all-vegetable shortening or 1 tablespoon Crisco Stick
1 can (20 ounces) pineapple chunks in pineapple juice, drained; reserve juice
2/3 cup cider vinegar
1/2 cup packed brown sugar
2 tablespoons soy sauce
4 teaspoons cornstarch
2 tablespoons water

## Directions

Heat oil in deep fryer to 350 degrees F.

## Drumstick Directions

In a small bowl, stir in the egg, water and milk.

In a large bowl, mix together the flour, tablespoon of cornstarch and cornmeal, baking powder. Next, add the ingredients from the small and mix until the batter becomes smooth.

Take several of the drumsticks and dip in the batter until well covered. Drop in deep fryer basket in oil and fry for 14-15 minutes. You want the drumsticks to be brown and crisp on the outside, and tender on the inside. Remove from oil and place on paper towels.

## Pineapple Sauce Directions

As the chicken drumsticks are frying, you can prepare the pineapple sauce. In a large saucepan, melt the Crisco on medium heat.

Stir in the onion and green pepper and sauté for 3-4 minutes. Mix in the pineapple juice, vinegar, brown sugar and soy sauce and stir together.

In a small bowl, mix together the water and cornstarch. Pour it into the large saucepan and stir continuously. Next, add in the pineapple chunks and bring to boiling. Stir occasionally for 2 minutes.

Add the sauce over the drumsticks. You can use some of the sauce over some cooked rice for an excellent meal.

Makes approximately 4 servings.

# Johnny's Beer Battered Chicken Strips

## Ingredients

   1 egg, beaten
   3/4 cup beer
   1 cup all-purpose flour
   1 teaspoon baking soda
   1 teaspoon salt
   ground black pepper
   3 chicken breast halves; skinless, boneless

## Directions

In a large bowl, add in the egg, beer, flour, salt, pepper and baking soda. Stir until well combined. Cover bowl and let it sit for 30 minutes.

Heat oil in deep fryer to 365 degrees F.

Cut chicken breasts into 1-inch wide strips. Dip into batter and coat well before placing them in small batches into deep fryer. Fry for 1-2 minutes or until golden brown on bottom. Turn strips over and fry another minute or until both sides are golden brown. Remove from oil and drain on paper towels before serving.

Serve with your favorite dipping sauces.

Makes approximately 4 servings.

# Russian Chicken Kiev

## Ingredients

4 large boneless, skinless chicken breasts
1 teaspoon salt
1/3 cup butter or margarine
1 tablespoon minced parsley
1 teaspoon lemon juice
1 clove garlic, minced
1/3 cup all-purpose flour
1-1/2 cups dry bread crumbs
2 eggs, beaten

## Directions

On a cutting board, slice the chicken breasts in half. Take the salt and sprinkle over the chicken.

In a small bowl, add in the butter parsley, garlic and lemon juice. Stir until well mixed and spread 2 teaspoonfuls all along the center length of each chicken half. Next, tuck in each end and the longer sides all around the butter. Use a skewer to keep closed.

In two small bowls, add the bread crumbs to one and the flour in the other. In a third bowl, beat in the eggs.

Take each chicken breast piece and dip in the flour first, then the egg and finally the bread crumbs. Put the chicken seam-side down on a platter or large plate and place in refrigerator for 3 hours.

Heat oil in deep fryer to 365 degrees F.

Place chicken in deep fryer for 5 minutes or until golden brown and fork tender. Remove from oil and place on paper towels before serving.

Makes approximately 4 servings.

# Mississippi Curried Chicken Squares

## Ingredients

18 slices soft white bread
3 tablespoons soft bread crumbs
1 (5 oz.) can chunk white chicken or 3/4 cup minced cooked chicken
1/4 cup roasted shelled peanuts
1/4 cup minced green onion
1/8 teaspoon 5-spice powder or allspice
1 teaspoon curry powder
1/4 teaspoon sugar
Pinch of pepper
1 teaspoon soy sauce
2 tablespoons chopped parsley
1 egg yolk, slightly beaten

## Directions

Take the bread and remove all of the crust from around each slice. Put the crust in one bowl and cover with a towel so that it stays soft.

Using your blender, blend the bread crusts into crumbs. Do only a few at a time.

Heat oil in deep fryer to 375 degrees F.

In a medium bowl, add 3 tablespoons of the crumbs, chicken, green onion, peanuts, allspice, curry, sugar, pepper, parsley and soy sauce. Stir the ingredients until well combined.

Take the bread slices that you used in removing the crusts and roll each one with a rolling pin until flattened. Cut the flattened square in half. Use a teaspoon to scoop out a spoonful of filling and place on one bread half. Place the other half on top and pinch to seal them together.

Brush the squares with the egg yolk and drop 2-3 at a time in deep fryer basket. Fry for 1 minute 45 seconds. Turn the squares halfway through. Remove from fryer and place on paper towels before serving.

Makes approximately 4-6 servings.

# Virginia Style Fried Peanut Chicken Strips

## Ingredients

1 1/2 cups finely chopped roasted peanuts
1/4 cup cornstarch
1/2 teaspoon sugar
1/4 teaspoon powdered ginger
2 tablespoons lemon juice
2 egg whites, lightly beaten
2 whole boneless and skinless chicken breasts

## Directions

Heat oil in deep fryer to 375 degrees F.

Mix together the cornstarch, sugar and ginger in a small bowl and stir until mixed together. Add the lemon juice and egg whites and mix thoroughly. Set aside for now.

In a pie pan, put in the chopped nuts and set aside.

Take the chicken breasts and cut into nice thin slices. Next, dip the chicken slices in the bowl with the egg mixture. Then, take and roll it through the chopped nuts.

Drop 3-4 chicken strips in deep fryer for 2 minutes or until nicely golden brown. Remove from oil and put on some paper towels to drain. Serve with your favorite dipping sauces.

Makes approximately 4 servings.

# Louisiana Cajun Fried Fish

## Ingredients

    2 pounds of fish fillets
    3 eggs, slightly beaten
    1/2 cup milk
    1/2 cup beer
    3 tablespoons prepared mustard
    1/2 to 1 teaspoon Tabasco sauce
    2 tablespoons salt, divided
    2 teaspoons black pepper, divided use
    1/2 to 1 teaspoon cayenne pepper, divided use
    3 cups fine yellow corn flour

## Directions

In a large bowl, stir in the eggs until slightly beaten. Add the beer, milk, mustard, Tabasco sauce and 1/2 of both the salt and pepper. Stir until mixed.

Next, take the fish fillets and cut them into smaller bite size chunks and add them to the bowl. Roll them in the mixture until well coated. Cover the bowl with a lid or plastic wrap and put in the refrigerator for one hour.

After 45 minutes, heat oil in deep fryer to 370 degrees F.

On a large plate, combine the rest of the salt and pepper with the corn flour and stir until mixed.

Take fish out of the refrigerator and roll the pieces in the corn flour mix. Drop fish in fryer and deep fry until they begin to float to the top of the oil. They should be golden brown when you remove them.

Let the fish drain on paper towels before serving.

Makes approximately 4 servings.

# Dan's Deep Fried Lobster Fritters

## Ingredients

1 1/2 cups cooked minced lobster meat
1 1/3 cups all-purpose flour
2 teaspoons baking powder
1/4 teaspoon paprika
1 egg, beaten
2/3 cup milk
1/4 teaspoon salt

## Directions

Heat oil in deep fryer to 375 degrees F.

In a large bowl, add the flour, salt, baking powder and paprika and combine. In a separate medium bowl, stir together the beaten egg and milk. Add the lobster meat and stir.

Pour the lobster bowl into the flour bowl and stir until well blended.

Using a tablespoon, scoop out spoonfuls and drop in deep fryer. (Fry in small batches of 4-5) Fry for 5 minutes or until golden brown. Remove from fryer and drain on paper towels before serving.

Makes approximately 4 servings.

# Midwest Deep Fried Catfish

## Ingredients

      1 1/2 lbs. catfish meat
      1/2 cup all-purpose flour
      1/2 cup yellow cornmeal
      1 teaspoon salt
      1/2 teaspoon pepper
      1/2 cup milk

## Directions

Heat oil in deep fryer to 375 degrees F.

In a large bowl, add in the flour, cornmeal, salt and pepper. Combine until well mixed.

In a small bowl, pour in the milk.

Take catfish and dip in milk bowl, then into the flour bowl, coating completely.

Add small batches to deep fryer and fry for 2 minutes. Turn fish over and fry another 2 minutes or until golden brown. Remove from fryer and place on paper towels to drain before serving.

Makes approximately 4 servings.

# Fish Sticks - Taco Style

## Ingredients

>1 package (9 oz.) frozen fish sticks
>1/4 cup taco sauce
>1/2 cup shredded Monterey Jack cheese

## Directions

Heat oil in deep fryer to 370 degrees F.

Deep fry fish sticks for approximately 3 minutes or until golden brown. Remove from fryer and place of paper towels to drain excess oil.

Turn on broiler in your stove. Place the fish sticks on a broiler plate. Pour a little of the taco sauce over the top of the fish sticks and sprinkle on some of the cheddar cheese.

Broil in oven for 1-2 minutes or just until cheese is melted. Serve immediately.

Makes approximately 4 servings.

# Deep Fried Atlantic Cod

## Ingredients

1 lb. frozen cod
1 egg
3/4 cup flour
1/2 cup water
1 teaspoon salt
1 tablespoon sesame seed

## Directions

Thaw frozen cod.

Heat oil in deep fryer to 375 degrees F.

In a large bowl, add the egg, flour, salt, sesame seeds and water. Stir until well mixed.

Pat down the cod with paper towel. The batter will not stick properly if the pieces are wet.

Dip cod into the batter and put in deep fryer for 3 minutes. Flip the fillet over and continue frying for another 3 minutes. Remove when golden brown. Drain on paper towels before serving.

Makes approximately 4 servings.

# Fried Crab Pinwheels

## Ingredients

6 cooked frozen or canned crab
1 tablespoon lemon juice
1 (8 oz.) package cream cheese, softened
1/4 teaspoon garlic salt
1/8 teaspoon white pepper
1/4 cup finely chopped water chestnuts
1/4 cup finely chopped green onions
60 wonton wrappers
1 egg white, lightly beaten

## Directions

Heat oil in deep fryer to 360 degrees F.

Drain and rinse off the crab before shredding. Use the lemon juice to sprinkle a bit over the top of crab.

In a medium bowl, combine the cream cheese with the garlic salt and white pepper. Mix until it becomes creamy and smooth. Add in the crab, chestnuts and onions and quickly stir.

In each of the wonton wrappers, place a teaspoon amount of the crab mixture in the center. Then, use the egg white and a brush to brush each edge of the wrapper. Bring up the wrapper edges and pinch together so that they resemble a pinwheel.

Add 4-5 wrappers to deep fryer and fry for 2-3 minutes or until they turn golden brown. Remove from fryer and drain on paper towels before serving.

Makes approximately 12 servings.

# Breaded Butterfly Shrimp

## Ingredients

     1 lb. large shrimp, peeled and deveined and butterflied
     1 quart water
     1 1/2 cups cornstarch
     2 eggs, beaten
     2 cups fresh bread crumbs

## Directions

Heat oil in deep fryer to 350 degrees F.

Mix together the cornstarch, eggs and water in a large bowl. Stir until well combined. In a small bowl, add the bread crumbs.

Take each shrimp and dip it first into the cornstarch mixture, coating thoroughly. Next, add it to the breadcrumb bowl and coat it completely. Repeat the process for a second time so that you have double-coated each shrimp.

Deep fry small batches of 3-4 shrimp in fryer until golden brown. Remove from oil and drain on paper towels before serving.

Makes approximately 4-6 servings.

# Northeast Deep Fried Flounder

## Ingredients

8 flounder fillets, skin removed
1/2 gallon whole milk
1 cup pancake mix
1 cup cornmeal
lemon wedges

## Directions

Heat oil in deep fryer to 370 degrees F.

In a large baking dish or pan, add the flounder and pour enough milk over them to completely cover them up.

Add the cornmeal and pancake mix to a medium bowl and stir until combined.

Drain off the milk from the flounder and then place in the cornmeal bowl. Coat both sides completely and place one fillet at a time into deep fryer. Fry fillets for approximately 4 minutes or until golden brown on both sides, turning them over one time.

Remove from oil and place on paper towels to drain oil. Serve with lemon wedges. Add a few parsley sprigs for an extra touch.

Makes approximately 8 servings.

# Mike's Deep Fried Razor Clams

## Ingredients

4 large razor clams, cleaned and dried
1 (4 oz.) packet saltine crackers, finely crushed
1/2 teaspoon ground black pepper
1/4 teaspoon ground cayenne pepper
1/4 teaspoon paprika
1/4 teaspoon garlic powder
2 eggs, beaten

## Directions

Heat oil in deep fryer to 375 degrees F.

Add the crackers, paprika, garlic powder and both peppers to a small bowl and stir until combined. In a separate small bowl, add the beaten eggs.

Take clams and dip them first into the egg bowl, then run them through the cracker bowl, coating thoroughly.

Place clams in deep fryer and fry until golden brown. Do not overcook. Remove from oil and drain on paper towels before serving.

Makes approximately 4 servings.

# Pub Style Beer Battered Fish Fillets

## Ingredients

2 lbs. cod fillets
1 cup all-purpose flour
1 teaspoon salt
1 teaspoon baking powder
3/4 cup beer
1/2 cup milk
2 eggs, beaten

## Directions

Heat oil in deep fryer to 375 degrees F.

Add the baking powder, salt and flour in a large bowl and stir with a wooden spoon until combined. Mix in the beaten eggs, milk and beer, stirring until it becomes a smooth batter.

Dip cod fillets in batter and coat completely. Place them on a baking pan to stand for 10 minutes.

Place small batches of fillets in deep fryer and fry until golden brown on bottom. Turn each one over and continue frying until the bottom also becomes golden brown. Remove from fryer and drain on paper towels before serving.

Makes approximately 8 servings.

# Pacific Deep Fried Shrimp

## Ingredients

1 lb. medium shrimp, peeled (tails left on) and deveined
1/2 teaspoon salt
1/2 teaspoon ground black pepper
1/2 teaspoon garlic powder
Old Bay seasoning
1 cup all-purpose flour
1 teaspoon paprika
2 eggs, beaten
1 cup panko crumbs

## Directions

Heat oil in deep fryer to 375 degrees F.

In a medium bowl, add the shrimp, pepper, garlic powder and salt. Stir to combine.

Add the flour and paprika to a small bowl and quickly combine. Add beaten eggs to another small bowl. Use a third separate bowl for the breadcrumbs.

Take each shrimp and dust them with Old Bay seasoning before coating in the flour bowl. Next, run it through the egg bowl, and finally, coat them in the breadcrumb bowl.

Add small batches in deep fryer and fry 4 minutes or until golden brown. Remove from oil and place on paper towels to drain excess oil.

Makes approximately 4 servings.

# Steve And Al's Deep Fried Oysters

## Ingredients

12 oz. shucked oysters, drained
1/2 cup all-purpose flour
1 teaspoon salt
1/2 teaspoon ground black pepper
2 eggs, lightly beaten
3/4 cup fine breadcrumbs

## Directions

Heat oil in deep fryer to 375 degrees F.

In a small bowl, add the flour, salt and pepper and combine. Add the beaten eggs to another small bowl. Finally, add breadcrumbs to a third small bowl.

Take oysters and dip first in the flour bowl, then into the egg bowl, and roll in breadcrumb bowl to coat thoroughly.

Add small batches to deep fryer and fry for 2 minutes or until golden brown. Remove from oil and set on paper towels to drain before serving.

Makes approximately 4 servings.

# Old Fashioned Fried Hush Puppies

## Ingredients

2 cups cornmeal
2 teaspoons baking powder
1 teaspoon salt
1 whole onion, minced
2 tablespoons bacon fat
1 egg
2/3 cup milk

## Directions

Heat oil in deep fryer to 350 degrees F.

In a large bowl, add corn meal, salt and baking soda. Stir until combined.

In a medium pan, heat the bacon fat and sauté the onion in it. Sauté until limp, but do not overcook.

Beat egg in a bowl and add to large bowl of flour mixture. Add the milk and sautéed onion. Stir entire mixture until it becomes a nice batter.

Form 3 inch round balls and deep fry 2-3 minutes or until they become golden brown. Remove from oil and drain on paper towels before serving.

Makes approximately 4 servings.

# Soft Shell Crab – Deep Fried

## Ingredients

6 soft-shell crabs
1 cup milk
Salt and pepper
Parsley, minced, fresh
1 egg, beaten
1 cup all-purpose flour
1 lemon, cut into 6 slices

## Directions

Heat oil in deep fryer to 375 degrees F.

Thoroughly wash and clean the six crabs.

In a medium bowl, mix in the egg, milk, salt and pepper. Stir until well combined. Add the crabs and let sit in the bowl for a couple of minutes.

Take out the crabs and then dip into bowl of flour.

Deep fry crabs for several minutes until you see them turn golden brown in color. Remove from fryer and drain on paper towels. Serve with lemon slices and parsley.

Makes approximately 6 servings.

# Atlantic Tuna Croquettes

## Ingredients

2 tablespoons butter
1/4 cup all-purpose flour
3/4 teaspoon salt
1/8 teaspoon pepper
1 cup milk
2 cans (7 oz. each) tuna, drained
2 tablespoons chopped parsley
1/2 teaspoon lemon juice
1 cup fine dry bread crumbs
1 egg, lightly beaten
2 tablespoons water

## Directions

Melt the butter in a large saucepan. Next, add flour, salt and pepper and stir until well combined.

Stir in the milk and constantly stir until it becomes thick. Add in the tuna, parsley and lemon juice to the pan, stirring until well mixed. Chill the mixture in the refrigerator for 2 hours.

Heat oil in deep fryer to 375 degrees F.

Take mixture out of refrigerator and form the dough into 8 different croquettes.

In two small bowls, combine the egg and water in one, and the bread crumbs in another. Roll the croquettes into the bread crumbs, then into the egg mixture and back through the bread crumbs.

Add to deep fryer two at one time and fry for approximately 5 minutes or until golden brown. Remove from oil and drain on paper towels before serving.

Makes approximately 4 servings.

# Philadelphia Fried Oysters

## Ingredients

12 large oysters
1 cup all-purpose flour with salt and pepper added
1 egg, beaten
1 jar mayonnaise
1 cup soft bread crumbs
Tartar sauce

## Directions

Heat oil in deep fryer to 375 degrees F.

Combine the flour, salt and pepper in a small bowl. After patting dry the oysters, roll them in the flour mixture.

In 3 small bowls, add mayonnaise to one, the beaten egg to another and the breadcrumbs to the third one.

Dip the oysters first into the mayo bowl, then into the crumbs, then into the egg bowl. Finally, run them through the crumbs again.

Deep fry for 1-2 minutes or until you see the oysters turn golden brown. Fry 3-4 at one time. Remove from fryer and drain on paper towels. Serve with tartar sauce.

Makes approximately 6 servings.

# Deep Fried Mexican Chimichangas

## Ingredients

1 lb. ground beef, browned and drained
1 medium onion, chopped
1/2 cup enchilada sauce
12 flour tortillas
2 cups cheddar cheese
2 cups shredded lettuce
2 cups chopped green onions

## Directions

Heat oil in deep fat fryer to 375 degrees F.

Add the ground beef to a large pan and brown. Drain in strainer and add the beef to a large bowl. Combine the onion and enchilada sauce with the beef and mix.

Lay out a flour tortilla and spoon out 3 tablespoons full of the meat in the middle of the tortilla. Fold the tortilla chimichanga style and use toothpicks to keep it together.

Drop the tortilla in deep fryer for approximately 2 minutes, turning once halfway through. Tortilla should be golden brown. Remove from oil and letting drain on paper towel.

Serve with your favorite garnishes such as cheese, onion, lettuce, guacamole, etc.

Makes approximately 4 servings.

# Aunt Candy's Fried Spinach Balls

## Ingredients

2 cups chopped cooked spinach
2 tablespoons butter
2 tablespoons grated onions
2 tablespoons grated cheese
salt and pepper
2 eggs, divided use
2 cups breadcrumbs, divided use
1/8 teaspoon allspice
1/4 cup water

## Directions

Heat oil in deep fryer to 365 degrees F.

In a large bowl, add the chopped spinach, salt, pepper, melted butter, onion, cheese, allspice, 1 egg and 1 cup breadcrumbs. Mix together until well combined and then let sit for 5-10 minutes.

Form mixture into 1-inch balls.

In two small bowls, use one for the remaining cup of breadcrumbs. In the second bowl, stir together the remaining egg and 1/4 cup of water.

Take spinach balls and coat in breadcrumbs. Then dip in the egg bowl before running them through the breadcrumbs a second time.

Add small batches of spinach balls to deep fryer and fry until golden brown. Remove from oil and place on paper towels to drain excess oil before serving.

Makes approximately 12 servings.

# Southern Deep Fried Okra

## Ingredients

8 oz. Okra
1/2 cup yellow corn meal
1/2 teaspoon paprika
1/4 teaspoon ground red pepper
1/4 teaspoon salt
5 drops hot pepper sauce
1 egg
1 tablespoon water

## Directions

Heat oil in deep fryer to 360 degrees F.

On a cutting board, slice off the stems and the tips from the okra. Set aside for now.

In a large bowl, combine the corn meal, paprika, ground red pepper, salt and pepper sauce (if desired). Stir until well combined.

Next, beat in the egg and water in a small bowl. Add the mixture to the large bowl and stir. Take the okra and dip it into the batter. Be sure to cover the okra completely.

Deep fry for 1 minute and 30 seconds or until golden brown. Remove from oil and allow to drain on paper towels before serving. Use your favorite dipping sauces if desired.

Makes approximately 4 servings.

# Deep Fried Cucumbers

## Ingredients

1 cucumber
Salt and pepper
Cracker crumbs
1 egg, beaten
Salad oil

## Directions

Heat oil in deep fryer to 390 degrees F.

On cutting board, peel and slice cucumber from top to bottom in 1/4 inch slices. Use paper towels to pat dry the cucumber slices.

In a small bowl, beat egg. In another small bowl, add the cracker crumbs. Take the slices and dip them into the cracker crumbs, then into the egg bowl, and finally back through the cracker crumbs again.

Put in deep fryer until they turn golden brown. Remove from fryer and drain on paper towels before serving.

Makes approximately 4 servings.

# Diane's Deep Fried Cauliflower

## Ingredients

1 head cauliflower, washed and broken into bite-size flowerets
2 eggs, beaten
1 tablespoon milk
1/4 teaspoon salt
1 1/2 cups flour
2 tablespoons shredded parmesan cheese
1/4 teaspoon garlic powder
1/2 teaspoon dried thyme
1 teaspoon dried oregano
1/8 teaspoon paprika
1 dash cayenne pepper
1/4 teaspoon black pepper

## Directions

Heat oil in deep fryer to 365 degrees F.

In a large gallon storage bag, add in the eggs, milk and salt. Zip it shut and shake.

Take a second bag and combine the cheese, flour, thyme, garlic powder, oregano, cayenne, paprika and black pepper. Zip the bag shut and shake the ingredients.

Next, take the cauliflower flowerets and first add them to the bag with the egg mixture and shake to coat.

Then, put the cauliflower in the second bag and shake it until the cauliflower is well coated.

Add a batch of the cauliflower to deep fryer and fry for 5-6 minutes. You want them to be golden brown before removing. Use paper towels to drain excess oil and season with salt and pepper to taste.

Serve with a dipping sauce. Cocktail sauce works and tastes great with this recipe!

Makes approximately 6 servings.

# Texas Style Fried Green Tomatoes

### Ingredients

      3 - 4 large green tomatoes
      2 cups all-purpose flour
      1 tablespoon salt
      1 tablespoon pepper
      1 tablespoon Lawry's seasoned salt
      2 eggs
      2 cups milk

### Directions

Heat oil in deep fryer to 350 degrees F.

Take green tomatoes and slice in 1/2 inch slices.

In a medium size bowl, add the flour, salt, pepper and seasoned salt. Mix together for 15 seconds.

In another medium bowl, beat in the eggs and add the milk. Stir until well mixed.

Take each tomato slice and put it in the milk mixture. Then, put it in the flour mixture. Next, repeat this very same process once again to the same tomato slice.

Add 2-3 of these battered tomato slices to the deep fryer and fry for approximately 5 minutes or until you see them becoming golden brown. Remove from fryer and drain on paper towels before serving.

TIP: You can also substitute corn meal or cracker crumbs for the flour if you prefer.

Makes approximately 6-8 servings.

# Deep Fried Corn Fritters

## Ingredients

3 large eggs
1/2 cup unsalted butter, melted
1/2 cup milk
2/3 cup all-purpose flour
1 tablespoon plus 2 teaspoons baking powder
1/2 cup brown sugar
1/4 teaspoon salt
1 lb. corn, thawed if frozen
7 ounces canned creamed corn

## Directions

Heat oil in deep fryer to 370 degrees F.

In a large bowl, mix in the eggs, butter and milk. Stir until creamy. Add in the flour, baking powder, brown sugar, salt and all of the corn. Stir until well combined.

Using a tablespoon, drop large scoops of the batter in deep fryer basket. Drop 5-6 at one time and fry until they turn golden brown. Remove from oil and let them drain on paper towels before serving.

Makes approximately 8 servings.

# Kids Corn Dogs

## Ingredients

    1 cup yellow cornmeal
    1 cup all-purpose flour
    1/4 teaspoon salt
    1/8 teaspoon black pepper
    1/4 cup white sugar
    4 teaspoons baking powder
    1 egg
    1 cup milk
    2 (16 oz.) packages beef hotdogs
    16 wooden skewers

## Directions

Heat oil in deep fryer to 375 degrees F.

Add the flour, cornmeal, sugar, baking powder, salt and pepper to a large bowl and stir until combined. Next, add in the milk and eggs and stir until well mixed.

Insert a wooden stick into each hotdog. Pour the batter into a tall glass and dip hotdogs into batter to coat.

Add 2-3 corn dogs to deep fryer at one time and fry for 3 minutes or until golden brown. Remove from fryer and place on paper towels to drain excess oil before serving.

Makes approximately 16 servings.

# Oklahoma Style Fried Bread

## Ingredients

3 cups all-purpose flour
1 tablespoon butter
1 teaspoon salt
2 tablespoon melted butter
2 teaspoon baking powder
3/4 - 1 cup warm milk
1 teaspoon sugar

## Directions

Mix together the flour, salt, one tablespoon butter, baking powder and sugar. Stir until well combined.

Slowly add the milk. You only want enough milk to create a soft dough. Knead dough on floured surface for 5-10 minutes or until soft and smooth.

Next, make 6-8 dough balls out of the dough and coat the tops with the melted butter.

Cover the dough balls with a towel and allow to stand for 45 minutes.

Heat oil in deep fryer to 370 degrees F.

Take the dough balls and flatten them to around 5 inches in diameter and 1/4 inch thick.

Drop the dough in deep fryer for one minute or until you notice turn golden brown. Flip over and continue frying until that side turns golden brown. Remove from fryer and drain on paper towels before serving.

Makes approximately 8 servings.

# Easy Deep Fried Chinese Fried Walnuts

## Ingredients

1 lb. shelled walnuts
1 cup granulated sugar
salt to taste

## Directions

Add walnuts and water to a large pot and bring to boiling for 2-3 minutes. Remove walnuts with a strainer and place in a medium bowl. Do not rinse nuts off. Add the sugar and stir until hot nuts are completely coated.

Heat oil in deep fryer to 375 degrees F.

Add small batches of nuts to deep fryer and fry for 4 minutes. Remove nuts from oil and drain on paper towels. Season with salt to taste and put nuts in serving bowl.

Makes approximately 12 servings.

# Ultimate Cajun Deep Fried Turkey

## Ingredients

3 gallons peanut oil for frying, or as needed
1 (12 lb.) whole turkey, neck and giblets removed
1/4 cup Creole seasoning
1 white onion

## Directions

Safety Tip: Never fry a turkey indoors. Be sure turkey is thawed and not frozen. Do not overfill the fryer with oil or the weight of the turkey will cause it to overflow and cause possible burns to the body or create a fire hazard. Follow all safety directions.

Add the peanut oil to the fryer and heat to 400 degrees F.

Thoroughly rinse the turkey and dry with a dish towel or some paper towels.

Rub turkey with Creole seasonings. Don't forget to rub it on the insides as well.

In fryer basket, add the whole onion and the turkey. Lower the turkey into the fryer oil very slowly. Do not rush this step. Be sure the entire bird is covered in oil.

Turkey should be cooked for 3:30 minutes for one pound. So, for a 12 pound turkey, you would fry it for 46 minutes. Use a meat thermometer to check the temperature of the meat in the largest part of the bird. It should be at least 175 degrees.

Remove turkey and allow it to drain before serving.

# Sri Lanka Fried Chiles

## Ingredients

24 dried cayenne or japones chiles
4 tablespoons salt
1 quart water

## Directions

Mix together the water and salt in a small bowl. Add the chiles to the bowl and let soak for 60 minutes.

Heat oil in deep fryer to 375 degrees F.

Deep fry chiles until they become crisp. Remove from fryer and put on paper towels. Salt to taste before serving.

Makes approximately 12 servings.

# Cherokee Fried Bread

## Ingredients

2 1/2 cups all-purpose flour
1 1/2 tablespoons baking powder
1 teaspoon salt
3/4 cup warm water
1 tablespoon vegetable oil
1 tablespoon nonfat dry milk powder
Cinnamon sugar

## Directions

In a large bowl, add the flour, baking powder and salt. Stir just until it becomes combined. Next, pour in the water, oil and nonfat dry milk. Stir until the mixture becomes a dough.

Lightly flour a work surface and take the dough from the bowl and roll on surface. Knead for 2-3 minutes into a smooth ball. Take a towel and cover the dough for 15 minutes.

Heat oil in deep fryer to 375 degrees F.

Take the dough and cut it into 8 different balls. Flatten each ball until it becomes 8-10 inches round.

Drop one dough round at a time in deep fryer. Fry 1-2 minutes on each side or until crisp. Remove from fryer and place on paper towels. Sprinkle with cinnamon sugar and serve.

Makes approximately 12 servings.

# Deep Fried Rabbit

## Ingredients

3 tablespoons milk
1 oz. all-purpose flour
1/4 teaspoon salt
1/4 teaspoon pepper
1 4 lb. rabbit, cleaned and cut into serving pieces
1 egg, lightly beaten
1 teaspoon water
3 oz. breadcrumbs
4 parsley sprigs

## Directions

In a small bowl, pour in the milk.

In a separate small bowl, combine the flour, salt and pepper, stirring until mixed.

Dip rabbit in the milk, then roll in flour mixture and set aside for 10-15 minutes.

Heat oil in deep fryer to 360 degrees F.

Deep fry rabbit approximately 15-20 minutes or until crisp and golden brown. Remove from fryer and drain on paper towels. Garnish with parsley and serve.

Makes approximately 4 servings.

# Twice-Fried Shredded Beef

## Ingredients

### Beef And Marinade Ingredients

3/4 lb. beef sirloin or flank steak
2 tablespoons dry sherry
2 tablespoons soy sauce
1 teaspoon sugar
1 teaspoon cornstarch
1 small carrot
1 green bell pepper
2 ribs celery
1 small onion

### Sauce Ingredients

2 tablespoons rice vinegar
1 tablespoon soy sauce
2 teaspoons sesame oil
1 teaspoon sugar
1/2 teaspoon chili oil
1/2 teaspoon cornstarch

## Beef Marinade Directions

Slice off excess fat from beef. Next, cutting across the grain, slice the beef into 1 1/2 inch pieces that look the size of matchsticks.

In large bowl, mix in all of the marinade ingredients and stir until well combined. Add the beef pieces into the marinade and let it stand for 30 minutes.

While beef is marinating, cut up the carrot, green pepper, celery and onion into similar 1 1/2 inch slices as the beef. Add them into a separate bowl for use later.

## Sauce Directions

In a medium bowl, add all of the sauce ingredients and stir until combined. Set aside for use later.

Heat 2 inches of oil in deep fryer to 375 degrees F.

Add half of the beef to fryer and fry for approximately one minute or until browned. Remove beef from oil and drain on paper towels. Fry the other half of the beef the same way.

In a skillet, add oil and fry the vegetables. Stir continuously and cook for one minute. Add the green pepper and celery and continue to cook another one minute. Finally, stir in all of the beef and the sauce, and stir well for another 30 seconds before serving.

Makes approximately 4 servings.

# World's Fair Corn Dogs

## Ingredients

6 all-beef hotdogs
1/2 cup yellow corn meal
1 cup all-purpose flour
1 teaspoon salt
1/4 teaspoon baking powder
1 cup milk
1 egg, beaten

## Directions

Heat oil in deep fryer to 375 degrees F.

In a medium bowl, add in the flour, corn meal, baking powder and salt. Stir until well combined.

Mix together the egg and milk in a small bowl and add to the corn meal mix. Stir until it becomes a batter.

Dip the hotdog into the batter and coat thoroughly. Drop 2 hotdogs at one time in deep fryer for 2-3 minutes or until it becomes golden brown.

Remove from fryer and place on paper towels to drain excess oil before serving.

Makes approximately 6 servings.

# Deep Fried Liver Strips

## Ingredients

1 pound calf liver
1 teaspoon salt
1 teaspoon dried leaf oregano
Dash pepper
1/4 cup olive oil
2 tablespoons lemon juice
Lemon wedges (optional)
Parsley (optional)

## Directions

Take the liver and cut it into strips measuring approximately 2 1/2 by 1/2 inches. Place the strips in a large bowl and shake the salt, pepper and oregano over all of them.

Pour in the lemon juice and olive oil. Mix in the bowl and coat over the liver strips. Next, cover with plastic wrap and place in refrigerator for 3 hours.

Heat oil in deep fryer to 365 degrees F.

Take liver out of refrigerator and drop a couple of strips in the deep fryer for 30 seconds or until they become brown. Remove from fryer and drain on paper towel. Garnish with lemon or parsley before serving if you wish.

Makes approximately 4 servings.

# Deep Fried Monte Cristo Sandwich

## Ingredients

12 slices white bread
8 slices Gruyère cheese
1/2 lb. sliced cooked ham
1 tablespoon plus 1 teaspoon prepared mustard
1/2 lb. sliced cooked chicken breast
Toothpicks
4 eggs, beaten
3/4 cup milk

## Directions

Heat oil in deep fryer to 400 degrees F.

On a slice of bread, add a cheese and ham slice. Next, spread on some of the mustard and add another piece of bread on top. Add a second cheese and ham slice along with part of the chicken breast. Top with another slice of bread.

Take a knife and cut the sandwich into quarters and stick toothpicks in the middle to secure sandwich.

In a small bowl, stir in the egg and milk. Then, dip each sandwich quarter in the mixture. Be sure to coat all parts of the sandwich.

Add several quarters to deep fryer basket and fry for 3 minutes and 30 second or until the pieces turn golden brown. Remove from fryer and drain on paper towels before serving warm.

Makes approximately 4 servings.

# Deep Fried Pineapple Rings

**Ingredients**

> 1 egg, beaten
> 1/4 cup flour
> 1 can (16 oz.) pineapple rings

**Directions**

Heat oil in deep fryer to 375 degrees F.

In a small bowl, add in beaten egg and flour, stirring until it becomes a thick batter.

Dip pineapple rings into batter and cover completely. Drop 2-3 rings into deep fryer and fry until golden brown. Remove from oil and drain on paper towels before serving.

Makes approximately 4 servings.

# Ed's Deep Fried Ribs

## Ingredients

6 lbs. beef ribs, cut into single rib pieces
2 tablespoons salt
3 tablespoons coarse ground black pepper
2 tablespoons cayenne pepper
2 tablespoons garlic salt
2 tablespoons onion salt
2 cups all-purpose flour
6 eggs, beaten

## Directions

Heat oil in deep fryer to 380 degrees F.

Combine the two peppers, salt, onion salt and garlic salt in a large bowl. In a separate bowl, add the flour. In another separate large bowl, add in beaten eggs.

Take ribs and hand rub the salt and pepper mixture onto them. Take your time and rub it in all over. Next, dip the ribs in the egg bowl and then into the flour bowl. Repeat the egg bowl to flour bowl once again.

Add 2-3 ribs to deep fryer basket and fry for 7 minutes. Remove from fryer and drain on paper towels before serving. You can use your favorite dipping sauces if desired.

Makes approximately 6 servings.

# Desserts

# Delicious Deep Fried Oreos

## Ingredients

1 large egg
1 cup milk
2 teaspoons vegetable oil
1 cup pancake mix
1 package cream-filled chocolate sandwich cookies (such as Oreo)

## Directions

Heat oil in deep fryer to 375 degrees F.

In a medium bowl, stir in the oil, milk and egg until well mixed. Gradually add the pancake mix to the bowl and stir continuously. Be sure you smooth out any lumps that may have formed.

Take each cookie and soak in batter until completely covered. Place in deep fryer in small batches. Fry for 2-3 minutes or until you see the cookies become golden brown. Place on paper towels to drain excess oil before serving.

Makes approximately 30 servings.

# Sue's Cinnamon Fried Ice Cream

## Ingredients

1/2 cup vanilla ice cream
2 tablespoons cinnamon
1/2 cup sugar
3/4 cup corn flakes (crushed)
3 tablespoons whipped cream

## Directions

In a small bowl, add in the sugar and cinnamon and quickly combine. In another small bowl, add in the corn flakes.

Next, scoop out the half cup of ice cream into one nice round ball. Roll it through the sugar bowl first, then into the corn flake bowl so that it covers the ice cream completely. Put the ice cream back in the freezer for 20-30 minutes.

Heat oil in fryer to 375 degrees F.

Remove the ice cream ball from the freezer. Quickly place in deep fryer for 15 seconds. Immediately remove, drain excess oil and add to a small dish.

Add whipped cream and serve.

Makes approximately 1 serving.

# Mom's Fried Apple Pies

## Ingredients

2 tablespoons butter
4 apples (peeled cored and sliced)
1/2 cup sugar
1/2 teaspoon cinnamon
1 teaspoon lemon juice
8 pieces biscuit dough (refrigerated flaky)

## Directions

In a large skillet, melt the butter over medium heat. Next, add in the apples along with the cinnamon, apples, sugar and lemon juice. Stir occasionally and cook for 13-15 minutes or until you see the apples become soft. Take off of stove and let cool.

Heat oil in deep fryer to 360 degrees F.

While you are waiting for the apple filling to cool down, flour a work surface or large cutting board and roll out the biscuits into circles that measure approximately 8 inches.

Use a tablespoon to scoop 3 spoonfuls of apple filling in a line down the middle of the biscuit. Moisten the outer circle edges with water, fold in half and seal with fingers or tines on a fork.

Add pie to deep fryer and fry each one separately for 7 minutes or until it becomes golden brown. Remove from fryer and place on paper towels to drain. Top with powdered sugar and serve.

Makes approximately 8 servings.

# Tasty Funnel Cakes

## Ingredients

3 eggs
2 cups milk
1 teaspoon vanilla extract
1/4 cup white sugar
3 2/3 cups all-purpose flour
1/2 teaspoon salt
2 teaspoons baking powder

## Directions

Heat oil in deep fryer to 375 degrees F.

Add the salt, baking powder and half of the flour to a small bowl and quickly stir until combined.

Add the vanilla, sugar, eggs and milk to a separate large bowl and mix well. Next, gradually add the ingredients in the flour bowl and continue stirring until you see the batter become smooth. NOTE: Do not get too thick, you want it to be able to pour out of the funnel.

Pour in 1/2 cup of the batter into the funnel. Be sure to keep your finger plugging up the bottom of the spout on the funnel. Remove finger over deep fryer and make circles with the batter.

TIP: An easier method to this is to use an old ketchup bottle to squirt the batter out into the fryer.

Fry just until the mixture becomes golden brown. Turn the funnel cake over and fry the other side 30-45 seconds. Remove from fryer and place on paper towels to drain. Add powdered sugar over the top and serve.

Makes approximately 12 servings.

# Deep Fried Pear Dessert

## Ingredients

4 Bartlett pears, cored and diced
1/2 cup white sugar
1 tablespoon cornstarch
2 teaspoons ground cinnamon
1 teaspoon lemon zest
1/2 cup graham cracker crumbs
1/2 cup chopped pecans
1 quart vanilla ice cream
6 (8 inch) flour tortillas
1/4 cup honey
1 teaspoon ground cinnamon
1 tablespoon white sugar

## Directions

Heat oil in deep fryer to 375 degrees F.

Add tortilla shells to deep fryer by adding them one at a time. As they are lying flat in the oil, take a wooden spoon and gently press down in the middle of the shell to create a sort of "cup". Fry until it becomes golden brown and then turn over to fry other side for 30-45 seconds. Remove from fryer and drain on paper towels.

In a medium saucepan, add in the pears, cinnamon, cornstarch, sugar and lemon. Stir until well mixed and then heat on medium until it begins to boil. Reduce heat and let cook for 1-2 additional minutes before removing from heat and allowing to cool.

In a separate small bowl, mix together the pecans, 1 teaspoon cinnamon and the crumbs. Next, get 6 nice sized scoops of ice creams and roll each one in the crumb bowl.

In each tortilla shell, brush it with honey and sprinkle some cinnamon and sugar over it. Now take the covered ice cream balls and place in individual tortilla shells. Then, take the pear mixture in the saucepan that has cooled completely, and add it over the ice cream before serving.

Makes approximately 6 servings.

# Aunt Sherry's Deep Fried Cinnamon Strips

## Ingredients

1 cup sugar
1 teaspoon cinnamon
1/4 teaspoon nutmeg
10 (8 inch) flour tortillas

## Directions

Heat oil in deep fryer to 375 degrees F.

In a one-gallon sealable food bag, mix together the cinnamon, sugar and nutmeg.

Take the flour tortillas and slice them into 1-inch wide strips. Place 5-7 strips at a time in the deep fryer for 30-40 seconds. Strips should be a golden brown color. Turn them over and fry another 30 seconds before removing from fryer and draining on paper towels.

Next, add the cooked strips to the sugar bag and toss 5-10 seconds until well coated before serving.

Makes approximately 36 servings.

# Fast And Easy Fried Elephant Ears

## Ingredients

1 1/2 cups sugar
2 teaspoons cinnamon
10 (8 inch) flour tortillas

## Directions

Heat oil in deep fryer to 360 degrees F.

In a medium bowl, mix together the sugar and cinnamon until combined.

Add one tortilla at a time to deep fryer and fry for 20-30 seconds or until golden brown. Turn it over and fry for another 15 seconds before removing from fryer. Do not overcook. Place on paper towels to drain.

Brush one side of the tortilla with butter and then sprinkle with generous amounts of cinnamon and sugar. Serve warm.

Makes approximately 8 servings.

# Hun Yang Thai Fried Bananas

## Ingredients

    3/4 cup white rice flour
    1/4 cup tapioca flour
    2 tablespoons white sugar
    1 teaspoon salt
    1/2 cup shredded coconut
    1 1/4 cups water
    8 bananas

## Directions

Heat oil in deep fryer to 370 degrees F.

Add in both flours, coconut, salt and sugar in a large bowl and mix until combined. Slowly add the water and stir continuously as you go until you get a nice batter.

Prepare bananas by first peeling them, then cutting them lengthwise in half. Cut each one lengthwise a second time so that each banana provides you with 4 pieces.

Add each banana to the batter and coat completely before placing in deep fryer. Fry for about one minute or until you see them become golden brown. Remove from fryer and put on paper towels before serving.

Makes approximately 16 servings.

# Classic Fried Sopaipillas

## Ingredients

4 cups all-purpose flour
2 teaspoons baking powder
1 teaspoon salt
4 tablespoons shortening
1 1/2 cups warm water
Cinnamon
Sugar
Honey

## Directions

Add the shortening, baking powder, flour and salt in a large bowl and mix together thoroughly. Then, slowly add the water and stir until the batter becomes doughy and smooth. Cover with a lid or plastic wrap for 15-20 minutes so that is sets up.

Heat oil in deep fryer to 375 degrees F.

Get a cutting board or a solid work area and flour the surface. Set the dough from bowl on surface and roll it out to where it is approximately 1/4 inch thick. Next, use a square cookie cutter or a knife to cut 3-4 squares out of the dough.

Drop 1 square at a time in deep fryer until you see one side become golden brown. Turn the other side over and continue frying for about 15 seconds until it becomes golden brown as well. Remove from fryer and use paper towels to drain excess oil.

Serve by themselves, or sprinkle cinnamon and sugar over the top. You can also dip in honey or serve with vanilla ice cream to create some awesome tasty treats.

Makes approximately 24 servings.

# Caramel Apple Delights

## Ingredients

3/4 + 1/3 cups sugar
1 + 1/2 teaspoon ground cinnamon
2 apples, peeled, cored and diced
1 (8 oz.) package cream cheese, softened
2 tablespoons caramel ice cream topping
1/2 teaspoon vanilla extract
9 (7 inch square) egg roll wrappers
1 tablespoon cornstarch
1 tablespoon water

## Directions

Heat oil in deep fryer to 375 degrees F.

Add the 1/2 teaspoon cinnamon and 3/4 cup sugar to a pie pan and quickly stir until combined.

Next, combine the teaspoon of cinnamon, 1/3 cup sugar and all of the softened cream cheese in a large bowl and stir until well mixed. Add in the vanilla extract along with the caramel topping and stir until combined. Finally, stir in the diced apples.

Get the wrappers and set each one on a flat work area. Using a tablespoon, or teaspoon, scoop out 2-3 spoonfuls of apple mixture onto each wrapper. (If using teaspoon, scoop out 5-6 spoonfuls.)

In a separate small bowl, stir in the water and cornstarch. Use a brush to moisten the edges around the wrapper before rolling each one up and sealing.

Add 1-2 wrappers to deep fryer and fry for approximately 5 minutes or until you see them turn a nice light brown color. Remove from fryer and drain on paper towels.

Take each apple wrapper and sprinkle on some cinnamon sugar before serving.

Makes approximately 9 servings.

# Ultimate Deep Fried Twinkies

## Ingredients

6 Twinkies (frozen)
6 wooden sticks (for putting into Twinkies)
1 cup milk
1 tablespoon white vinegar
1 tablespoon oil
1 cup all-purpose flour
1 teaspoon baking powder
1/2 teaspoon salt
Flour for dusting

## Directions

In a small bowl, add in the milk, vinegar and oil. Mix together the flour, baking powder and salt in a separate large bowl. Next, slowly add the ingredients from the small bowl, stirring continuously until well combined. Place the bowl into your refrigerator for 15 minutes.

Heat oil in deep fryer to 400 degrees F.

Take wooden sticks and place one in the bottom of each Twinkie. Lightly dust the Twinkie with flour. Then, coat the Twinkie in the bowl taken out of the refrigerator.

Place 1-2 Twinkies at a time into deep fryer for 2-3 minutes. Twinkies will be done when you see them turning golden brown. Do not overcook. Remove from oil and drain on paper towels before serving.

Makes approximately 6 servings.

# Old Fashioned Apple Fritters

## Ingredients

> 1 1/2 cups all-purpose flour
> 1 tablespoon white sugar
> 2 teaspoons baking powder
> 1/2 teaspoon salt
> 2/3 cup milk
> 2 eggs, beaten
> 1 tablespoon vegetable oil
> 3 cups apples, peeled, cored and chopped
> 1 cup cinnamon sugar

## Directions

Heat oil in deep fryer to 375 degrees F.

Quickly combine the sugar, flour, salt and baking powder in a large bowl. Then, add the beaten eggs, oil and milk. Stir until everything is well mixed together. Finally, add the apples and gently stir until mixed in evenly.

Using a tablespoon, scoop out spoonfuls and add to deep fryer. Fry small batches of 4-5 fritters for 2-3 minutes or until one side is golden brown. Turn the fritter over and continue frying for another minute or until it also turns golden brown. Remove from fryer and place on paper towels.

Sprinkle on the cinnamon sugar and serve.

Makes approximately 24 servings.

# Apricot Fruit Filled Empanadas

## Ingredients

4 cups chopped dried apricots
1 1/2 cups water
3/4 cup white sugar
1 teaspoon ground cinnamon
1 teaspoon ground nutmeg
Dash ground cloves

1 (1/4 oz.) envelope active dry yeast
1 cup lukewarm water
1/4 cup shortening or lard
3 cups all-purpose flour
1 teaspoon salt

## Directions

Prepare the apricots by adding them to medium saucepan with 1 1/2 cups of water. Bring to boil, reduce heat and continue cooking until the fruit becomes tender, which is approximately 12-15 minutes. Once tender, take away from heat and let cool for 5-10 minutes.

Next, add the apricots to your blender along with the water from the saucepan, nutmeg, cinnamon, sugar and cloves. Set the blender to puree and blend.

In a separate large bowl, add in one cup of water. Pour out the yeast packet over the top of the water and let stand for 5-7 minutes. Then, stir in the salt, shortening and flour. Continue stirring until the dough strengthens.

Heat oil in deep fryer to 370 degrees F.

Now, knead the dough for 6 minutes before rolling it out to a quarter inch thickness. Use a cookie cutter (The top of a large round glass can also be used as a template) to cut out dough.

In the center of each piece of round dough, add one tablespoon of the apricot mixture. Fold over and seal the empanada before adding it to the deep fryer.

Fry until the bottom becomes golden brown. Turn it over and deep fry the other side until it becomes golden brown as well. Remove from fryer and put on paper towels to drain the excess oil before serving.

Makes approximately 18 servings.

# Chocolate Covered Strawberry Fritters

## Ingredients

1 cup all-purpose flour
1/4 cup unsalted butter, melted
1/4 cup heavy cream
3 eggs
1/4 teaspoon salt
2 tablespoons packed brown sugar
1 teaspoon ground cinnamon
2 cups hulled strawberries
1 cup semisweet chocolate chips
3 tablespoons butter
1 teaspoon vanilla extract
1/4 cup heavy cream
2 tablespoons confectioners' sugar for dusting

## Directions

Heat oil in deep fryer to 365 degrees F.

Mix in the cream, butter, eggs, brown sugar, cinnamon and salt in a large bowl. Stir or whisk until the mixture is well combined. Next, mix in the strawberries, but be careful not to tear them up.

To make the chocolate sauce, take a large microwavable bowl and add in the 3 tablespoons of butter, vanilla, chocolate chips and the cream. Mix them together until combined and then microwave on high for 45 seconds. Stir the mixture and if chips are not yet melted, heat another 20 seconds and stir again. Set aside when melted.

Add the coated strawberries in small batches to deep fryer. Fry for 30-45 seconds or until they become golden brown. Turn them over and fry other side until golden brown. Remove from fryer and drain. Sprinkle with confectioner's or powdered sugar before serving with the chocolate sauce.

Makes approximately 8 servings.

# Fall Pumpkin Funnel Cakes

## Ingredients

    1 1/2 cups all-purpose flour
    1/4 teaspoon baking powder
    1 teaspoon baking soda
    1 teaspoon cinnamon
    1/4 teaspoon salt
    1 egg, beaten
    1/4 cup packed brown sugar
    3/4 cup canned pumpkin puree
    1 cup milk
    3/4 teaspoon pumpkin pie spice
    1/2 cup confectioners' sugar for dusting

## Directions

Heat oil in deep fryer to 375 degrees F.

In a large bowl, combine the flour with the cinnamon, baking powder, baking soda, pumpkin spice and salt.

In a separate large bowl, add the beaten egg, milk, puree and brown sugar. Mix until it is well combined. Next, slowly start adding in the flour bowl mixture, stirring continuously as you go. You want to stir until you get a smooth batter.

Use a funnel or better yet, an old ketchup bottle that can be used to squirt the batter into the fryer. If using a funnel, fill it up with batter and keep your finger over the spout. Release finger over fryer and make small circles with the batter. The goal is to create a spiral sort of design.

Fry for 30-60 seconds or until you see the mixture turn golden brown. Turn it over and do the same thing for the other side. Remove from oil and place on paper towels to drain. Add confectioner's sugar over the top to taste before serving.

Makes approximately 4 servings.

# Island Coconut Puffs

## Ingredients

3/4 cup all-purpose flour
1/2 cup self-rising flour
1/2 teaspoon ground cinnamon
1/2 teaspoon ground cardamom
1/4 cup white sugar
1 1/2 cups coconut milk

## Directions

Heat oil in deep fryer to 375 degrees F.

Combine the two flours, sugar, cinnamon and cardamom in a large bowl. Quickly stir.

Slowly add the coconut milk and stir continuously until the batter becomes smooth and without lumps.

Using a tablespoon, scoop out spoonfuls and place in deep fryer. Fry for 2-3 minutes or until they become golden brown on the outside. Remove from oil and put on paper towels so excess oil can drain off.

Makes approximately 4 servings.

# Beth's Banana Spring Rolls

## Ingredients

    2 large bananas or plantains
    8 (7 inch square) spring roll wrappers
    1 cup brown sugar

## Directions

Heat oil in deep fryer to 375 degrees F.

Prepare the bananas by peeling them and then slicing them lengthwise into 4 different pieces.

Next, lay out a wrapper and place one of the lengths of banana across it diagonally. Add brown sugar over the top of the banana as desired. Roll up the wrappers to the center, moisten the edges and seal.

Add 2-3 bananas at a time to deep fryer. Fry for 2-3 minutes or until banana wrappers become golden brown. Remove from oil and drain on paper towels before serving.

Makes approximately 8 servings.

# Deep Fried Applesauce Doughnuts

## Ingredients

3 tablespoons butter, softened
3/4 cup sugar
3 eggs
1 cup applesauce
1 teaspoon vanilla extract
4 1/2 cups all-purpose flour
3 1/2 teaspoons baking powder
1 teaspoon salt
1/2 teaspoon ground cinnamon
1/4 teaspoon ground nutmeg
1/4 cup milk
Additional sugar for sprinkling

## Directions

Heat oil in deep fryer to 380 degrees F.

Add the sugar and butter to a large bowl and stir continuously until it becomes creamy. Next, beat in the eggs until well combined. Add the vanilla and applesauce and stir until mixed.

Slowly add the flour, stirring as you go. Then mix in the baking powder, cinnamon, nutmeg and salt and stir thoroughly. Add a little of the milk at a time to the batter while stirring until thick.

Using a teaspoon, scoop out spoonfuls of batter and place in deep fryer. Do small batches at a time. Fry for approximately 1 minute per side or until the doughnuts become golden brown all over. Remove from fryer and place on paper towels to soak up excess oil.

Sprinkle or roll doughnuts in sugar before serving.

Makes approximately 60 doughnuts.

# Deep Fried Mexican Fritters

## Ingredients

1 cup water
2 1/2 tablespoons sugar
1/2 teaspoon salt
2 tablespoons vegetable oil
1 cup all-purpose flour
1/2 cup sugar
1 teaspoon ground cinnamon

## Directions

Heat oil in deep fryer to 375 degrees F.

Add the 2 1/2 tablespoons of sugar, oil, salt and water to a medium saucepan and bring to a boil on medium heat. Turn off heat.

Next, gradually add the flour to the mixture and continue stirring until you get a ball like dough. Then, use a pastry bag to add strips of dough to fry in deep fryer, or roll out the dough and cut the strips with a knife if you don't have a pastry bag.

Add small batches of strips to fryer and fry until they become golden brown. Remove from oil and let them drain on paper towels for a minute or two.

In a small bowl, add in the cinnamon and sugar. Take the strips and run them through the bowl to coat before serving.

Makes approximately 8 servings.

# Classic Deep Fried Ice Cream

## Ingredients

1 quart vanilla ice cream
1 loaf white bread
1/2 cup sugar
2 teaspoons cinnamon

## Directions

Take a cookie sheet or baking pan and put it in your freezer for several hours to get cold.

Scoop large balls of ice cream and put them on the cold cookie sheet. Place the sheet back in the freezer for one hour.

To prepare the ice cream for frying, remove the outer crust from 2 slices of bread. Sit an ice cream ball on top of one slice and put the second slice over the top. Pick the bread and ice cream up and work the bread slices around the ice cream ball. Be sure to cover all parts of the ball. When finished, place the ice cream back into the freezer for 20-30 minutes.

Heat oil in deep fryer to 375 degrees F.

Take one ice cream ball at a time out of the freezer and place it in deep fryer. Fry for 15 seconds or until golden brown, turning as you fry. Remove from oil and place on paper towels adding the cinnamon and sugar over the ice cream and serving.

Makes approximately 6 servings.

# Easy Deep Fried Snickers Bars

## Ingredients

>Snicker candy bar
>Popsicle stick (or other stick)
>Funnel cake mix

## Directions

Press in the popsicle or other type of stick into the bottom of the Snickers bar. Slide it up approximately halfway so that it will not slip out.

Place the candy bar in the freezer for at least 2 hours to harden.

Heat oil in deep fryer to 375 degrees F.

While oil is heating, mix the funnel cake mix in a medium bowl. Remove Snickers bar from freezer and dip into batter.

Add to deep fryer for about 2 minutes or until it becomes golden brown. Remove from oil and drain on paper towels before serving. (Tip: Sprinkle with powdered sugar for an added treat.)

Makes approximately 1 serving.

# Special Cranberry Sauce Fritters

## Ingredients

13 oz. cranberry jelly slices
2 cups all-purpose flour, divided use
2 tablespoons sugar
Dash salt
1 teaspoon baking powder
1 cup water

## Directions

Open can of cranberry slices and carefully lay them out on a baking sheet that has been lined with parchment paper. You do not want them to stick to the surface. Put the sheet in the freezer for 4-5 hours until the slices are frozen.

Heat oil in deep fryer to 375 degrees F.

Get out 2 separate medium sized bowls and add 1 cup of flour to the first bowl. In the second bowl, mix together the sugar, baking powder, salt and the rest of the flour. Next, add in the cup of water and stir continuously until you get a nice smooth batter. Then let it stand for about 10 minutes.

Take cranberries out of freezer and place one at a time in the flour bowl first. Then put it in the batter bowl and cover completely. Add 2 cranberry rings at a time into the deep fryer. Fry for 2-3 minutes or until they become golden brown. Remove from oil and drain on paper towels before serving.

Makes approximately 4 servings.

# Farm Fresh Fried Apple Rings

## Ingredients

4-5 apples
1 egg, beaten
1/4 cup milk
1/2 cup flour
1 teaspoon baking powder
1 dash salt
5 teaspoons cinnamon
2 teaspoons powdered sugar

## Directions

Prepare apples by washing them off and then cutting them into individual rings about 1/4 inch thick. With 4-5 apples you should get around 13-15 rings.

Heat oil in deep fryer to 375 degrees F.

In a large bowl, add in the milk, beaten egg, salt, flour and baking powder. Stir until the well combined.

Take the cinnamon and sprinkle it over the top and bottom of each apple ring. Next, take each ring and cover it in the batter bowl.

Add 3 rings at a time into the deep fryer and fry for 1minute on each side or until the rings turn golden brown on both sides. Remove from oil and place on paper towels to drain excess oil.

Sprinkle powdered sugar over the tops of the apple rings and serve. (Tip: You also serve with whipped cream or even your favorite jelly if you like.)

Makes approximately 13-15 servings.

# Deep Fried Apricot Cream Pies

## Ingredients

1 1/3 cups water
6 oz. apricots (dried)
1/4 cup sugar
2 tablespoons cream cheese, softened
15 oz. refrigerated piecrusts

## Directions

Heat oil in deep fryer to 360 degrees F.

In a medium saucepan over medium heat, add the water and apricots. Bring to boiling and continue to cook for 25 minutes. When finished, remove from heat, drain the water and then mash the apricots. Let them sit to cool.

In a blender or food processor, add in the cream cheese and sugar and blend until the ingredients become smooth. Next, put in the apricots and blend just until well combined.

Take out the piecrusts and use a rolling pin to make them into 12 inch circles. Next, cut out 4 inch circles from each of the piecrusts. Then take a teaspoon and scoop out 2 teaspoonfuls of the apricots on one half of each circle. Use your fingers to fold over the circle and seal the edges. You may need to moisten the edges with water.

Add 1-2 apricot pies to deep fryer and fry for 4-5 minutes, turning them over halfway through. Pies should be golden brown on both sides. Remove from oil and drain on paper towels before serving.

Makes approximately 18 servings.

# Fried Watermelon

## Ingredients

10 lbs. watermelon
11 tablespoons flour
7 tablespoons cornstarch
2 egg whites, beaten
powdered sugar

## Directions

Heat oil in deep fryer to 390 degrees F.

In a large bowl, combine the flour, cornstarch and beaten egg whites. Stir until well mixed.

Prepare watermelon by cutting into smaller squares and removing all of the pulp and seeds. Dip the pieces into the flour mixture and coat both sides.

Add the watermelon to deep fryer in very small batches and fry until the outside becomes golden brown. Turn piece over and fry it to golden brown as well. Remove from oil and drain on paper towels before serving.

Tip: Try adding some powdered sugar for a sweeter tasting watermelon.

Makes approximately 12 servings.

# Honey Fried Dipples

## Ingredients

2 cups honey
1 cup water
2 tablespoons sugar
6 eggs, beaten
1 teaspoon vanilla extract
2 3/4 cups flour
1/3 cups vegetable oil, divided
cinnamon
1 cup chopped nuts

## Directions

Heat oil in deep fryer to 360 degrees F.

In a medium saucepan, add the water, honey and sugar. Bring to boiling and continue cooking for 12 minutes. Reduce heat to low and leave there until later.

In a large bowl, add in the beaten eggs and vanilla. Stir until combined. Next, gradually stir in the flour and then add the oil. Continue stirring until you get the mixture to become a dough.

Take the dough and divide it into 5 equal sections. Then use a rolling pin on one section at a time and roll out to where it is thin. Cut 2 inch by 4 inch pieces from the dough. Roll each one into a circle.

Add small batches of dough circles to deep fryer and fry to golden brown. Remove from oil and place on paper towels to drain excess oil.

Take each dipple and dunk it into the honey sauce mixture in saucepan. Add cinnamon and nuts over the top and serve.

Makes approximately 12 servings.

# Chocolate Lovers Wontons

## Ingredients

1 (12 oz.) package wonton wrappers
1 cup milk chocolate chips
10 strawberries, quartered
1/4 cup confectioners' sugar

## Directions

Heat oil in deep fryer to 360 degrees F.

Use a teaspoon to scoop out a spoonful of chocolate chips and add them to the middle of a wonton wrapper. Add one piece of the quartered strawberries to the top and then fold up the wrapper. Moisten the edges and seal it as airtight as you can.

Add small batches of wonton wrapped chocolates to deep fryer. Fry for 30-45 seconds or until golden brown. Turn each one over and fry another 20 seconds before removing from fryer. Place on paper towels to drain excess oil.

Sprinkle confectioner's sugar over the tops of the chocolate wrappers and serve.

Makes approximately 40 servings.

# Sheryl's Deep Fried Cherry Pies

## Ingredients

   1 cup all-purpose flour
   1/4 teaspoon baking powder
   1/4 teaspoon salt
   2 tablespoons shortening
   1/3 cup boiling water
   1 cup cherry pie filling
   1/4 cup maple syrup - optional
   1/4 cup whipped topping - optional

## Directions

Heat oil in deep fryer to 370 degrees F.

Add together the flour, salt and baking powder in a medium bowl. Stir until combined. Mix in the shortening and stir until it begins looking like crumbs. Then, slowly add the boiling water until you get the mixture moist and dough like.

Add the dough to a floured cutting board and knead it approximately 6-8 times. Next, create four equal sections from the dough. Use a rolling pin to roll the dough out to form an 8 inch circle.

Add 1/4 cup of cherry pie filling to the middle of each dough circle. Then fold the dough over and seal the edges with your fingers.

Add one cherry pie at a time to the deep fryer and fry for 2 minutes or until golden brown. Turn the pie over and fry for another 2 minutes or until golden brown. Remove from oil and place on paper towels before serving. Tip: Can be served with whipped cream or syrup for a unique taste.

Makes approximately 4 servings.

# Kiss Me Chocolate Wontons

## Ingredients

24 milk chocolate kisses
8 oz. chocolate chips
24 wonton wrappers
Confectioners' sugar

## Directions

Heat oil in deep fryer to 375 degrees F.

Lay out a wonton wrapper and add one of the chocolate kisses to the middle of it. Then place 4-5 chocolate chips around the kiss.

Fold up wrapper and moisten edges. Press the edges together to seal.

Add small batches of chocolate wrappers to deep fryer. Fry for 45-60 seconds or until they become golden brown. Turn them over halfway through. Remove from fryer and place on paper towels.

Sprinkle confectioner's sugar over the top before serving.

Makes approximately 12 servings.

# Carmela's Italian Cookies

## Ingredients

1 tablespoon sugar
1 teaspoon grated lemon peel
1 teaspoon vanilla extract
1/2 teaspoon salt
4 eggs, beaten
2-1/2 cups all-purpose flour
1 cup honey
Candy sprinkles - optional

## Directions

Heat oil in deep fryer to 360 degrees F.

Add the salt, vanilla, sugar and lemon peel into a large bowl and stir until combined. Add in the beaten eggs and mix together. Next, slowly add the flour, stirring continuously until you have a smooth dough.

Lightly dust a cutting board and use it to knead the 1/2 cup flour into the dough. Then cut the dough into 20 pieces and roll each one out into the shape of a pencil. Then cut each "pencil" into 3 unique pieces.

Place small batches of 4-5 into deep fryer and fry for 2 minutes or until the cookies turn golden brown. Flip them over and fry for 1 minute or until golden brown. Remove from fryer and put them on paper towels to drain excess oil.

Heat the honey in a microwave safe bowl and drizzle over cookies. Add some cute candy sprinkles for a decorative touch before serving.

Makes approximately 60 cookies

# Grammies Fried Apple Rings

## Ingredients

3/4 cup all-purpose flour
1 egg, beaten
1/4 cup maple syrup
1/4 cup buttermilk
3 large apples, peeled, cored, and cut into 1/4-inch rings
Confectioners' sugar

## Directions

Heat oil in deep fryer to 380 degrees F.

Add the beaten egg, flour, buttermilk and syrup to a medium bowl and stir until well combined.

Take prepared apple rings and coat them thoroughly in the batter. Add 2-3 apple rings at one time into deep fryer for 1-2 minutes or until you see them turn golden brown. Remove from fryer and place on paper towels.

Sprinkle confectioner's sugar over the top before serving.

Makes approximately 4 servings.

# Fried Sugar Apple Fritters

## Ingredients

2-1/2 cups all-purpose flour
1/2 cup nonfat dry milk powder
1/3 cup sugar
2 teaspoons baking powder
1 teaspoon salt
2 eggs, beaten
1 cup water
2 cups chopped peeled apples
Sugar

## Directions

Heat oil in deep fryer to 375 degrees F.

Stir together the flour, sugar, dry milk, salt and baking powder in a large bowl until combined. Add the beaten eggs and water, stirring until mixed. Finally, add the apples and mix evenly in batter.

Using a teaspoon, scoop a spoonful of batter and drop in deep fryer in small batches. Fry for 1-2 minutes on each side or until they turn golden brown. Remove from oil and place on paper towels to drain excess oil.

Pour sugar in a small bowl and dip apple fritters in bowl before serving.

Makes approximately 40 servings.

# Mexican Peach Chimichangas

## Ingredients

2 flour tortillas (6 inches), warmed
2 tablespoons cream cheese, softened
1 snack-size cup (4 oz.) diced peaches, drained
1/8 teaspoon ground cinnamon
Whipped cream, caramel ice cream topping, powdered sugar - optional

## Directions

Heat oil in deep fryer to 380 degrees F.

Lay out flour tortillas and top them with the softened cream cheese. Add peaches in the middle of the tortilla and then sprinkle cinnamon over the top. Fold in the sides and then the ends just like a regular chimichanga.

Add one chimichanga at a time to deep fryer and fry for 2-3 minutes, turning over halfway through. Chimichanga should be golden brown all the way around. Remove from oil and place on paper towels to drain oil.

Tip: Add your favorite toppings to chimichangas such as whipped cream, honey, caramel or powdered sugar.

Makes approximately 2 servings.

# Grandma's Special Doughnuts

## Ingredients

>    1 (10 oz.) can buttermilk biscuit dough
>    1 cup confectioner's sugar or powdered sugar

## Directions

Heat oil in deep fryer to 380 degrees F.

Take biscuits out of package and place on a cutting board or other work surface. Cut out holes in the center of each biscuit.

Add 2-4 doughnuts to deep fryer at a time. Fry for 2-3 minutes or until they turn golden brown. Turn each doughnut over and fry other side until golden brown as well. Remove from oil and drain on paper towels.

Sprinkle powdered sugar or confectioner's sugar over the top before serving.

Makes approximately 10 servings.

# Italian Carnival Pastries

## Ingredients

1/2 teaspoon salt
1 teaspoon vanilla extract
1 1/2 tablespoons sugar
3 large eggs, beaten
1 (5 oz.) can evaporated milk
1/2 teaspoon vanilla extract
3 1/2 cups all-purpose flour
Confectioner's sugar

## Directions

In a large bowl, add the sugar, salt and beaten eggs. (Stir with wooden spoon until well combined. You can use an electric mixer if you have one as well.) Next, mix in the milk and vanilla, stirring until combined. Slowly stir in the flour and mix for 5 minutes into a smooth dough. The dough should not stick to the bowl. Remove and cover with a towel for 15-20 minutes.

Heat oil in deep fryer to 360 degrees F.

Divide the dough into smaller pieces and use a rolling pin on a floured surface to create long thin strips in the 6x2 inch range. Lay out the strips and slice a small 2 inch line down the center. Grab hold of the bottom edge and draw it up and through the slit.

Add 2-3 pieces at one time to deep fryer and fry for 2 minutes or until they become golden brown. Remove from fryer and drain on paper towels. Add confectioner's sugar over the tops before serving.

Makes approximately 24 servings.

# Deep Fried French Croquignoles

## Ingredients

1/3 cup softened butter
1 cup sugar
1 teaspoon vanilla
1/2 teaspoon grated lemon peel
4 eggs, beaten
3-3/4 cups all-purpose flour
1-1/3 tablespoon baking powder
3/4 teaspoon freshly grated nutmeg
1/2 teaspoon salt
1/2 cup light cream
1/2 cup confectioner's sugar

## Directions

Add the 4 beaten eggs in a large bowl. Stir in the butter, sugar, vanilla and lemon peel and stir continuously. You want a nice creamy mixture.

In another large bowl, add in the flour, nutmeg, salt and baking soda. Stir just until it becomes mixed together. Pour this flour mixture slowly into the batter bowl. Stir constantly as you add more flour. The goal is to get a soft, smooth dough.

Put a cover or towel over the bowl and place it in your refrigerator for 3 hours. It needs time to firm up.

Heat oil in deep fryer to 365 degrees F.

Remove the dough from the refrigerator and cut it into 4 distinct pieces. Lightly flour a work area on your counter or table. Use a rolling pin to roll out the dough until it is approximately 1/4 inch thick.

TIP: Work with one section of dough at a time and leave the rest of the dough in your refrigerator so that it stays firm.

Next, cut the dough into strips measuring about 6 inches long by an inch wide. Twist each strip 3-4 times and then connect the ends together. You may have to moisten the ends to make them stick together.

Deep fry in oil for 1 minute 30 seconds and turn over to fry the other side. The croquignoles should be golden brown when finished. Remove from fryer and place on paper towels to drain.

Serve croquignoles with confectioner's sugar sprinkled over the top.

# Scrumptious Banana Doughnuts

## Ingredients

2 1/2 cups Flour
2 1/2 teaspoon baking powder
1/2 teaspoon baking soda
1/4 teaspoon nutmeg
1/2 teaspoon salt
2 eggs
1/2 cup honey
1 banana, mashed
2 tablespoons butter or margarine
1/2 cup sour cream
1/2 teaspoon vanilla

## Directions

In a medium bowl, add the flour, baking powder, baking soda, nutmeg and salt. Stir until well combined.

In a large bowl, beat in eggs one at a time. Slowly pour in the honey while continually stirring. Add the mashed banana, sour cream, butter and vanilla and mix well.

Gradually add the flour mix to the large bowl, stirring as you go until you have a soft dough. Leave dough in bowl, cover and place in refrigerator for 2-3 hours.

Heat oil in deep fryer to 370 degrees F.

Roll out dough to 1/4 inch thickness on a lightly floured work surface or cutting board. Cut dough with a doughnut cutter.

Add 2-3 doughnuts to deep fryer and turn once when the doughnuts rise to the top of the fryer. Brown and remove from fryer. Place on paper towels to drain. Serve warm.

# Salvation Army Style Doughnuts

## Ingredients

2 tablespoons vegetable shortening
1 cup sugar
2 eggs, beaten
4 3/4 cups flour
2 teaspoons baking powder
1 teaspoon salt
3/4 cup milk
1/2 teaspoon nutmeg
1/2 teaspoon vanilla

## Directions

Heat oil in deep fryer to 375 degrees F.

In a large bowl, add the shortening and sugar. Stir until the mixture becomes smooth and creamy. Mix in the eggs and vanilla, stirring until well combined.

In a medium bowl, mix the flour, baking powder, salt and nutmeg together. Gradually pour the flour mixture into the creamy mix. Stir constantly and add in the milk as you go. You'll end up with a smooth dough.

Lightly flour a cutting board or other work surface. Use a rolling pin to roll dough to 1/4 inch thick. Next, cut the dough into rounds, and cut out the centers as well. You can use a glass or cup as a tool. Roll the centers together into balls for donut holes.

Drop the donuts and donut holes in batches in your deep fryer. Fry until the bottom turns golden brown and then flip over for 30 seconds to a minute until the other side browns. Remove from fryer and let stand on paper towels to drain.

Sprinkle confectioner's sugar over the tops before serving.

# Al's Deep Fried Cherries

## Ingredients

1 lb. fresh ripe red cherries
1 cup all-purpose flour
1/4 cup sugar
1/3 cup milk
1/3 cup dry white wine
3 eggs
Confectioner's sugar
Cinnamon

## Directions

Heat oil in fryer to 375 degrees F.

Take cherries and wash in sink. Leave stems on cherries. Dry with a towel.

In a medium bowl, beat in the eggs. Next, add the flour, sugar, milk and wine. Stir until the mixture becomes a smooth batter.

Put cherries into the batter and coat them thoroughly. Place them in the fryer basket and deep fry until golden brown. Remove from oil and let drain on paper towels.

Top with cinnamon or confectioner's sugar before serving.

# Deep Fried Spam Strips

## Ingredients

12 oz. can SPAM
1 cup all-purpose flour
Dash of salt
1 egg, beaten
1/2 cup milk

## Directions

Heat oil in deep fryer to 350 degrees F.

Cut SPAM into strips approximately 1 inch wide and 1/4 inch thick and set aside.

Add the flour, salt, egg and milk into a medium bowl and stir until combined and thick in consistency.

Dip the SPAM strips in the batter and fry in small batches for 4 minutes. Turn the SPAM over halfway through. Remove from oil and drain on paper towels before serving.

Makes approximately 4 servings.

# Oddities

# Deep Fried Coca Cola

## Ingredients

2 cups all-purpose flour
1 teaspoon baking powder
2 eggs, lightly beaten
1 1/2 cups Coca Cola

## Topping:

1 cup Coca Cola syrup
whipped cream
maraschino cherries

## Directions

Heat oil in deep fryer to 375 degrees F.

Add the flour and baking powder in a medium bowl and stir until combined. Next, stir in the beaten eggs and slowly add the Coca Cola, stirring continuously until you get a smooth batter.

Fill a funnel with 1/2 cup of the batter, keeping your finger over the spout. Remove finger from funnel over deep fryer and pour out the batter in a circular pattern. (Tip: You can use a turkey baster or an old squeezable ketchup bottle instead of a funnel if you prefer.)

Fry in deep fryer for 45-60 seconds, then turn over and fry other side another 30 seconds or until golden brown. Remove from oil and place on paper towels to drain excess oil.

Top with syrup, whipped cream and a cherry before serving.

Makes approximately 6 servings.

# Out Of This World Fried Moon Pie

## Ingredients

> 2 Moon Pies
> 1 cup all-purpose flour
> 1/2 cup corn flour
> 1 dash baking soda
> Club soda, refrigerated
> Powdered sugar

## Directions

Heat oil in deep fryer to 380 degrees F.

In a small bowl, mix together the two flours and baking soda until well combined. Slowly pour in the chilled club soda and stir until it becomes a smooth batter.

Dip the Moon Pie into the batter and coat thoroughly. Add to fryer basket and lower into deep fryer. Fry until it becomes golden brown. Remove from oil and place on paper towels to drain excess oil.

Sprinkle generous amounts of powdered sugar over the top and serve.

Makes approximately 2 servings.

# West Texas Deep Fried Rattlesnake

## Ingredients

    1 rattlesnake cut into 3 inch pieces
    1/4 cup oil
    2 tablespoons lemon juice
    1 teaspoon salt
    1 egg, beaten
    1/2 cup milk
    1/2 cup self-rising flour

## Directions

In a large bowl with a lid, add in the rattlesnake pieces along with oil, salt and lemon juice. Stir until all pieces are covered and cover. Place in refrigerator for 8 hours or longer to marinate.

Heat oil in deep fryer to 375 degrees F.

In a medium bowl, add in the milk and beaten egg, stirring until combined. Then, stir in the flour until it becomes a smooth thin batter. Let stand for 15 minutes to set.

Remove rattlesnake pieces and dry with paper towels. Next, take each rattlesnake piece and dip into batter, covering the entire piece. Fry small batches in deep fryer until they turn golden brown. Turn each one over and fry opposite side. Remove from fryer and place on paper towels to drain before serving.

Servings are dependent on size of snake.

# Kids Deep Fried Pop-Tarts

## Ingredients

Pop tarts, any flavor
Pancake mix (add water only)
Confectioners' sugar or powdered sugar

## Directions

Heat oil in deep fryer to 360 degrees F.

Prepare the pancake mix using the box directions. Make enough of the mix for 6 pancakes.

Take each pop tart and coat it in the batter until it is completely covered. Add the pop tart to deep fryer and fry for 1 minute on each side or until golden brown. Remove from oil and place on paper towels to drain excess oil.

Top with confectioner's or powdered sugar and serve.

Makes approximately 4 servings.

# Southern Deep Fried Skunk

## Ingredients

2 skunks, skinned and cleaned, scent glands removed
1 teaspoon salt
2 egg yolks, beaten
3 cups milk
1 1/2 cups all-purpose flour
1/2 teaspoon salt
2 tablespoons baking powder

## Directions

Cut cleaned and prepared skunks into small strips and pieces suitable for deep frying.

In a large saucepan, bring water to boiling and add skunk meat. Reduce heat and cook for 35-40 minutes or until skunk becomes tender. Remove from heat and drain water.

In a large bowl, stir together the milk, flour, baking powder, salt and egg yolks. Batter should thicken as you stir.

Dip skunk strips and pieces in batter and coat. Place small batches at a time in deep fryer. Fry until golden brown and turn over to fry other side to golden brown. Remove from oil and drain on paper towels before serving.

# Arizona Cactus Strips

## Ingredients

4 to 6 large cactus pads, needles and spines removed
1 cup all-purpose flour
1-1/2 teaspoon salt, divided use
1/4 teaspoon pepper
3 eggs, beaten
1/2 cup milk
1 cup soft bread crumbs
3/4 cup saltine crumbs
1-1/2 teaspoon chili powder
1-1/2 teaspoon cayenne pepper
Picante sauce

## Directions

Heat oil in deep fryer to 380 degrees F.

Take prepared cactus pads and slice into 1/2 inch by 3-4 inch long pieces. Add pieces to a bowl of water to clean, then dry with paper towels and set aside for later.

In a medium bowl, stir in the flour, 1/2 teaspoon salt and the pepper until combined. In a second small bowl, combine the milk and beaten eggs. Stir until well mixed. Finally, in a third medium bowl, mix together the bread and cracker crumbs, cayenne pepper, salt and chili powder.

Take cactus strips and pieces and first dip in flour bowl, then into egg bowl, and then coat with crumbs in crumb bowl.

Add small batches to deep fryer and fry for 2 minutes or until they turn golden brown, turning over pieces halfway through. Remove from oil and use paper towels to drain excess oil before serving. Dip in picante sauce for a tasty snack or appetizer.

Makes approximately 12 servings.

# Cajun Fried Alligator Tail

## Ingredients

1 Alligator meat
1 teaspoon cayenne pepper, if desired
1/4 cup vinegar
1/4 cup all-purpose flour
1 cup corn meal
Salt and pepper to taste

## Directions

Take fresh alligator tail and cut into two inch long by one inch thick pieces.

Add the alligator pieces to a small bowl and pour on some of the vinegar, as well as sprinkle on salt and pepper to taste. You can also sprinkle on some cayenne pepper if desired. Leave in bowl for 30 minutes.

Heat oil in deep fryer to 400 degrees F.

In a one gallon bag, add in the corn meal and flour. Mix together. Next, add the alligator pieces to the bag and shake until well coated.

Fry in oil until the pieces become golden brown. Remove from oil and drain on paper towels before serving.

# Measurement Conversion Chart

Tablespoon/Teaspoon Conversion

    3 teaspoons = 1 Tablespoon
    1/2 Tablespoon = 1 and 1/2 teaspoons
    1 Tablespoon = 3 teaspoons

Tablespoon/Cup Conversion

    2 Tablespoons = 1/8 cup
    4 Tablespoons = 1/4 cup
    5 and 1/3 Tablespoons = 1/3 cup
    8 Tablespoons = 1/2 cup
    10 and 2/3 Tablespoons = 2/3 cup
    12 Tablespoons = 3/4 cup
    16 Tablespoons = 1 cup

# ~~~~~ **Favorite Recipes** ~~~~~

1. _____ Page _____

2. _____ Page _____

3. _____ Page _____

4. _____ Page _____

5. _____ Page _____

6. _____ Page _____

7. _____ Page _____

8. _____ Page _____

9. _____ Page _____

10. _____ Page _____

11. _____ Page _____

12. _____ Page _____

13. _____ Page _____

14. _____ Page _____

15. _____ Page _____

16. _____ Page _____

17. _____ Page _____

18. _____ Page _____

~~~~~ **NOTES** ~~~~~

~~~~~ NOTES ~~~~~

~~~~~ **NOTES** ~~~~~

16110515R00090

Made in the USA
Lexington, KY
05 July 2012